Raising the Next Generation to Serve

兴起新一代服事

曾振锚著 Reginald Tsang

Raising the Next Generation to Serve
兴起新一代服事

与曾叔叔闲聊 3

兴起新一代服事

作者 / 曾振锚
中文编辑 / 古志薇
设计排版 / Busybees Design Consultants Ltd.

版次 / 二零二零年十一月初版
©2020 曾振锚

国际书号：978-1-6312-9932-2

Coffee with Uncle Reggie 3
Raising the Next Generation to Serve

by Reginald Tsang
Chinese Editor / May Ku
English Editor / Mary Ann Lucas
Design/ Busybees Design Consultants Ltd.
Edition/ First edition, November 2020

ISBN : 978-1-6312-9932-2

I am grateful for our own next generation, Trevor and Olivia, for the many intriguing lessons I learned from watching them grow up into adulthood, for insights from fascinating interactions at different life stages, and for forgiveness for many uses of their stories for sermon material! My dear wife from youth, Esther, has supported and tolerated my many transitions with traditional Hakka Christian stoicism: all this would not have been possible without her decades of faithfulness and dedication to our Lord.

我感谢我们的孩子宪材和宪慈。我从观看他们成长的过程中学到许多有趣的经验，从和他们在不同人生阶段的有趣互动中学到很多深入见解，他们也宽容地面对我在讲道中使用他们的故事，我为这一切深表感激！我年轻时所娶的爱妻温粹英，以传统的客家信奉基督的坚忍，支持并容忍了我的许多转变：没有她数十年的忠诚和对我们的主的奉献，这一切都是不可能的。

Raising the Next Generation to Serve
兴起新一代服事

目录
Table of Contents

Foreword

As I read through the chapters, I smiled as I read them. The style is encouraging and full of energy. Uncle Reggie's treatment of how he began and maintained a missions emphasis in the church (and especially an Asian-American church) is full of inspiration, exhortation, and very practical tips. Well done! The examples chosen of real people's stories throughout the chapters are powerful. I believe the Lord will use these to stimulate the church for His glory among the nations. Bless you, Reggie! Grace and peace,

John Shindeldecker
Author of *Peacemaking*

The word "generation" occurs 84 times in the NIV Bible, sometimes duplicated in the phrase "generation to generation." How very important it is that "one generation will commend Your works to another." (*generation*, Psalm 145:4) Uncle Reggie is aware of the impact on youth from their older generation. He has witnessed it first-hand, for example, in Cincinnati, in Thailand, and in China.

John Bascom
Former missionary to the Philippines
Former Acting English-Speaking Congregation Minister, Cincinnati Chinese Church

I recommend this book to you. Dr. Tsang (Reggie) writes with creativity and passion. He has decades of experiences that he freely shares. But I think the thing I value the most is his heart for God. Prayer has been a key part of his life and the resulting relationship with God enables him to help others and share these writings with us. Thank you for your efforts, Reggie!

R. Mark Beadle, Ed.D.
CEO & Head of School
www.Sevenstar.org

序言

当我阅读这些文章时，我笑了。风格令人鼓舞，充满活力。曾叔叔对他在教会（尤其是美国亚裔教会）中如何开始和维持宣道重点的处理充满了灵感、劝勉和非常实用的技巧。做得好！每篇文章所选择的真人真事的示例都是有力的。我相信主会用这些来激励教会在万国中彰显祂的荣耀。振锚，祝福你！愿你蒙恩、得平安。

约翰·辛德尔德克

《和平》（Peacemaking）的作者

在 NIV 圣经中，"代"一词出现了 84 次，有时在"世世代代"（圣经新译本）一词中重复出现。"这代要对那代颂赞你的作为"是多么重要（"代"，诗篇一四五 4）。曾叔叔意识到老一辈对青年的影响，他亦在例如是辛辛那提、泰国和中国，亲眼目睹了它。

约翰·巴斯科姆

前菲律宾宣道士

前辛城教会英语堂代任牧师

我向你推荐这本书。曾医生（振锚）充满创意和激情。他拥有数十年的经验，可以尽情分享。但我认为我最珍视的是他对上帝的心。祷告一直是他生命中的关键部分，由此而与上帝建立的关系使他能够帮助他人并与我们分享这些文章。振锚，谢谢你的努力！

马克·比德尔，教育学博士

Seven Star Academy 首席执行官兼学校负责人

www.Sevenstar.org

Raising the Next Generation to Serve
兴起新一代服事

This book is a treasure trove of knowledge and wisdom about children's and youth ministries, from someone who has the experience of loving and caring for children and youth with a Christ-like love for almost 5 decades. But not only that, the book emphasizes important aspects of the type of church in which children should be growing up, a church where there is mentoring, a strong missions emphasis (both at home and abroad), and where church members are continually looking to the Lord in prayer for guidance that is according to His Word.

Elton Chu
Senior Pastor
Alhambra Chinese Christian Center
Los Angeles, California

In an ethnic church (or any church or ministry), does anything get done right without good leadership? Of course not! God uses effective leaders to grow His church, and effective leaders probably learn most of what "works" through everyday practical experience.

So, what is a leader? By definition a leader is one who goes before and has a group following to serve some stated calling or purpose. I have known, and served with a very effective church leader off and on for 50 years. He happens to be one of my best friends. He is affectionately known as "Uncle Reggie" (UR).

In this new book by UR you will be exposed to the guts of real leadership with a well-honed plan to grow God's Kingdom well. He does this by telling stories about how God worked through himself and others. If you are desirous of being involved in the rewarding dynamic of establishing and nurturing the growth of ethnic churches, then this book is written for you. Read on and expect to be inspired to the work.

This is no armchair philosophic tome. Through the chapters of Uncle Reggie's book the reader is not treated to the modern mantra of "let's-make-Christianity-successful", but to practical and divine wisdom that was wrought on the anvil of actual experience in the heat of hard labor to advance the

这本书是一个宝库，收藏了有关儿童和青年事工的知识和智慧。作者拥有将近 50 年爱护和关怀儿童及青年的经验，并拥有基督般的爱心。但不仅如此，这本书还强调了教会要具备哪些特质，让孩童在当中成长：这样的教会要提供属灵导师，强调（在国内外）宣道的重要性，教会成员也不断在祷告中寻找合乎上帝的道的指导。

朱璧邗牧师
中国信徒家庭教会
加利福尼亚州洛杉矶阿罕布拉

在一个族群教会（或任何教会或事工）中，如果没有良好的领导，有什么事情能做得对呢？当然没有！上帝利用有效的领导者来发展自己的教会，有效的领导者多半会通过日常实践经验来学习有效的事奉。

那么，领导者是怎样的？顾名思义，领导者是指先行者，有一群后继者跟随，以履行一些既定的呼召或目标。我认识一位非常有效的教会领袖，并断断续续与他一起工作了 50 年。他恰好是我其中一个最好的朋友。他被亲切地称为"曾叔叔"。

在曾叔叔的这本新书中，你将了解到一个真正的领导者的本质。他精心计画如何好好地发展上帝的国。他讲述上帝如何通过他和其他人工作的故事，以实现这个计画。如果你有动力参与建立和培育族群教会成长，那么这本书就是为你而写。请继续阅读，希望对你做这项事工有所启发。

这不是一本扶手椅哲学的大部头著作。通过曾叔叔这本书中的文章，读者不会被灌输"让我们把基督教变得成功"的现代口头禅，

Kingdom's presence. Although Reggie was an internationally recognized neonatologist, he focused on serving God through diverse ministries.

Churches were planted. Medical Services International was initiated, with teams of doctors serving in China, and also teams of Chinese doctors coming to Cincinnati to study medicine. Many VBSs were consistently held each year. Chinese students attending local universities were brought under the umbrella of the Chinese Church. Youth For All Nations, with a strong Asian missionary focus, gave rich opportunities for high school and college-age students to minister abroad.

Let me introduce you to the man and his leadership. UR's philosophy of ministry has consistently been to raise up a new generation of believers committed to serving Christ's interests. You will discover that his leadership was always focused on stimulating the growth of ethnic churches internationally as well as here in the States.

In a most interesting manner, UR offers a toolbox filled with practical and divine wisdom to equip the reader to join with Jesus in expanding Christ's Kingdom through churches.

What tools or working principles are in the toolbox?

1. Yes, adults in the church need edification and strong ministry focus. He gives much anecdotal insight in this arena.

2. But, all ministry must have a future component as well. So, there must be a strong commitment to children and youth and the bonus is that they are fun to work with, and they are the future!

3. These ministries require participating workers. UR learned to take the lead by inviting others to join in. He personally "took them by the hand" and led them into service providing support and training as needed. His personal one-on-one encouragement kept the whole process moving forward.

God really isn't into "recipe Christianity" because the Spirit must be free to inspire, instruct, energize, and call to ministry. But healthy churches grow progressively; there is logic to it, a succession of steps that believers go

而是接收到切实而神圣的智慧，那是由艰苦地扩展上帝的国度的真实经验锻炼得来的。尽管振锚是国际公认的新生儿学家，但他也常年专注于通过各种事工为上帝服务。

他帮助建立了很多教会。他发起了国际医疗服务组织，与多批医生在中国服务。还有多批中国医生来辛辛那提学习医学。每年在教会里都会举行许多暑期圣经班的活动。上当地大学的中国学生被带到华语教会的大伞之下。以亚洲宣道为重心的"万国青年"计画，为高中和大专生提供了很多出国服事的机会。

让我向你介绍这个人物和他的领导理念。曾叔叔的事奉理念一直是培养新一代致力于服务上帝旨意的信徒。你会发现，他的领导始终致力于促进世界各地和美国当地族群教会的发展。

曾叔叔以一种最有趣的方式提供了一个充满实践和神圣智慧的工具箱，使读者可以与耶稣一起通过教会扩展基督的国度。

工具箱中包含哪些工具或工作原理呢？

1. 是的，教会中的成年人需要造就和高度重视事工。他在这个领域提供了很多轶事。

2. 但是，所有事工小组也必须有未来的组成部分。因此，必须致力发展儿童和青少年的工作，而好处是：和孩子青少年们一起工作很有趣，并且他们就是未来！

3. 这些事工需要参与的工人。曾叔叔学会了通过邀请其他人加入来发挥带头作用。他亲自"牵着他们的手"，带领他们投入服事，并根据需要提供支援和培训。他个人的一对一鼓励使整个过程不断向前发展。

上帝真的不喜欢"食谱基督教"，因为圣灵必须自由地鼓舞、指导、激励和呼召人服事。但是，健康的教会会逐步成长。这是有

through at a practical level. UR sets these forth in an engaging, captivating way.

If you have a heart to reach the Chinese in particular, I trust you will be encouraged to pursue that vision whole-heartedly as Uncle Reggie did. Do these ministry ideas work? I believe the testimony of many thousands of Chinese believers (and others) that Reggie influenced from around the world will testify with a roaring – AMEN!

Bruce Chester
Former Chairman of the US Board, Medical Services International
Elder, Faith Evangelical Church, Cincinnati

The Psalmist encourages us to tell the works of our God to our children, and for them to teach these to the next generations (Psalm 78:5-7). God's steadfast love is bestowed to thousands and generations as we continue to love and trust him (Exodus 20:6). Generational faith is possible because the Lord God, being the God of Abraham, Isaac and Jacob, is the living God!

Dr. Reginald Tsang's third Coffee Book, *Raising the Next Generation to Serve*, is very relevant and much needed for this Post-Truth Era. It gives clear guidance to millennials seeking answers about their faith in the true God. For Asian believers, especially the Chinese in diaspora communities, who are searching for strategies for effective ministries in a new environment, the book serves as a practical and effective handbook.

I am privileged to know Reggie, and enjoy reading Uncle Reggie's stories. Back when both Rosa and I were pursuing postgraduate degrees at the University of Cincinnati and Hebrew Union College, respectively, we relished his pastoral care through the Cincinnati Chinese Church. Our son Jathniel, barely two then, enjoyed the books he encouraged the church kids to read; at one point Reggie even rewarded Jathniel for reading the most number of children books in one month! We were also privileged to be involved in youth and children ministries. We witnessed how the church grew from a small

道理的：信徒在实践中要经历一系列步骤。曾叔叔以引人入胜、迷人的方式阐述了这些内容。

如果你有特别想接触华人的心，我相信你会像曾叔叔一样全心全意地追求这一愿景。这些对事工的想法行得通吗？我相信受曾叔叔影响、来自世界各地成千上万的华人信徒（和其他人）会大声说：阿们！

布鲁斯·切斯特
前国际医疗服务机构美国委员会主席
辛辛那提 Faith Evangelical Church 长老

诗人鼓励我们将上帝的作为告诉我们的孩子，并让他们向下一代传授知识（诗篇七十八 5-7）。我们继续爱祂、守祂的诫命，祂必向我们发慈爱，直到千代（出埃及记二十 6）。信仰是可以一代传一代的，因为作为亚伯拉罕、以撒和雅各的主上帝，是永生的上帝！

曾振锚医生的第三本书《兴起新一代服事》，是非常切合这个后真理时代、也是它所急需的。这本书提供了明确的指导，让千禧一代能为他们对真神的信仰寻求答案。有些亚洲信徒，特别是侨民社区中的华人信徒，正在一个新环境中为有效的事工寻找策略；对他们来说，这本书是一本实用而有效的手册。

我很荣幸认识曾医生，也喜欢阅读曾叔叔的故事。当年我和秀美分别在辛辛那提大学和希伯来联合学院攻读研究生学位时，在辛城教会享受过他的牧养。我们的儿子 Jathniel（那时只有两岁）很喜欢他鼓励教会孩子们阅读的书；有一次，他甚至为 Jathniel 在一个月内阅读了最多儿童书籍而奖励他！我们也很荣幸参与过青年和

church to a church with several congregations, from one location to many locations. Above all, we also praise the Lord for raising many servants of God from the church.

I find the book to be bible-centered in giving clear principles for church ministries and how pastors should be properly honored as servants called by God. Reggie's stories describe many facets of how a church can successfully instill the love of God in the hearts of children and youth. May our Lord use this book for his glory and honor!

Joseph Shao, PhD
President Emeritus, Biblical Seminary of the Philippines
4th General Secretary, Asia Theological Association

When I received the phone call from Uncle Reggie to write a foreword for this book, I was very honored and excited.

I first met Uncle Reggie in 1999, the first time I went to the Cincinnati Chinese Church. He was just chatting with some young people. I observed that as he was speaking with these young people, they were all smiling and excited, and I could see that they really respected and honored Uncle Reggie. It was actually quite a surprise to me because I knew he was a very fine scientist and well recognized in the medical field, but he did not have any airs about him as he chatted with them and other friends at the church.

I soon realized that this person was very concerned about children, youth and missions. As I've known him for 20 years, his work and ministry have changed and impacted me greatly.

God has given the next generation to us and entrusted us to use our lives to influence their lives. The bible has said that "children are the inheritance from the Lord, and the fruit of the womb is our reward." So God has given us children in His grace and blessing. The best blessings are not material but spiritual. If a person doesn't treat his possessions in a wise way, he might see more importance in material things than life. If a man has the world of materials, but loses his children what benefits are there?

儿童的事工。我们目睹教会如何从一个小教会发展成为一个拥有数个分会的教会，从只在一个地方敬拜到在许多地方敬拜。最重要的是，我们还为上帝在教会中培养了许多仆人而赞美主。

我发现这本书是以圣经为中心，为教会的各种事工提供了明确的原则，又指引会众如何恰当地尊敬牧师为上帝召唤的仆人。振锚的故事描述了教会如何成功地把上帝的爱灌输到儿童和青少年的心中。愿我们的主使用这本书彰显祂的荣耀和荣誉！

邵晨光博士
菲律宾圣经神学院荣誉院长
亚洲神学协会第四任总干事

接到曾叔叔的电话，要我为他退休后的第三本书写序言，真的让我受宠若惊，但也让我兴奋。

我在 1999 年认识曾叔叔。那是我第一次到辛城教会，他正和许多年轻人聊天。我留意到这群年轻人脸上的笑容与表情，可以看出他们多么敬爱这位叔叔。这样一位大科学家、医学界的泰斗，竟然毫无架子地与来教会的朋友们聊天，真让我吓一跳。

我很快就知道他非常非常关心儿童、青少年和宣道的工作。我认识他至今 20 年了，他的工作和事奉深深地改变和影响了我。

上帝把下一代交给我们，信任我们用生命去影响生命。圣经上说："儿女是耶和华所赐的产业，所怀的胎是他所给的赏赐。"上帝按祂的恩福把儿女赐给我们。最好的福分不是属物质的，而是属灵的。如果一个人没有明智地看待他的产业，他可能会看重物质的产业过于生命的产业。人若得到全世界的物质，却失去他的儿女，有什么益处呢？

Even Socrates once said "you people of Athens go over all of Greece looking for gold but you lose your children, what good is that?" Jesus said, "If a man wins the whole world but he loses his life, what good is that?" When we use all our time, energy and sweat to do many things and accumulate lots of money, but indeed lose our lives, what can we bring away from this life? The things that we have accumulated are not worth what we have lost. What Socrates had said is that if you have so much material, but you lose your children what is the benefit?

Young parents, these wise sayings should remind us that even though we may have many material possessions, it is not worth it if we lose our spiritual possessions and the eternal spirit of our children. May the Lord revive us, illuminate us, and awaken us to true values. Children are created by the Lord through us: we are only caretakers, temporarily nurturing our children for the Lord.

God has placed these children in our care and we need to be responsible to God. What kind of possessions are the children? They can become good or bad, so we need to educate them to understand the truth as they grow up, so that they can become precious for the country, the conscience of the generation, witnesses for history, and recipients and proponents of Truth. Good education of the next generation is priceless, an excellent contribution to society.

May the Creator of all, the Spirit that touched Uncle Reggie, also touch all of us so that we can be serious in nurturing the next generation. Amen.

Peter Yang
Deacon, Restaurant Ministry Leader
Cincinnati Chinese Church

It is said Sunday mornings are the most segregated times of the week in the U.S. Bringing together different cultures is always a challenge. Bringing together different cultures to proclaim the Gospel – our sinfulness and need for a Savior – is nearly impossible. Thankfully, what is impossible

苏格拉底也曾经讲过一句话："雅典人哪，你们挖遍希腊的土地盼望得着黄金，却失去你们的儿女，有什么益处呢？"耶稣讲过："人若赚得全世界，赔上自己的生命，有什么益处呢？"当我们用尽时间、精神和血汗做了许多工作，赚了一堆钱以后，结果赔上自己的生命，死的时候还能带走什么？所赚到的还是得不偿失。苏格拉底说这句话的意义就是：你若得着很多物质的产业，却失去了你的儿女，又有什么益处呢？

年轻的父母，你要从这些伟人智慧的话中得到提醒：假如我们损失了灵性的产业和子女永远的灵魂，即使我们拥有许多物质，也完全不值得。求主复兴我们，光照我们，令我们苏醒，认识真正价值的所在。我们的孩子是上帝所造的，借着我们的身体把他们生下来；我们不过是一个照顾者，代替上帝把孩子养育起来。

上帝把儿女这份产业赐给我们，要我们向赐产业的上帝交代尽责。儿女是一份怎样的产业呢？是一个可好可坏的产业。所以，我们要好好教育他们明白真理，成为国家的珍宝，时代的良心，历史的见证人，真理的领受者和拥护者。对下一代施行良好的教育，就是对社会作出无价的贡献。

但愿创造万物的上帝、感动曾叔叔的圣灵，同样也来感动我们各人，让我们能认真培育下一代的年轻人。阿们！

杨华礼
辛城教会餐馆福音事工执事

据说周日早晨是美国一周中最分隔的时间。把各种不同的文化汇集一起始终是一项挑战。汇集不同的文化来宣扬福音——我们是有罪的并且需要救主——几乎是不可能的。值得庆幸的是，在人所

with man is possible with God. Reginald Tsang, or "Uncle Reggie", as he is so affectionately known, has spent much of his life watching God do that which seems impossible through the Cincinnati Chinese Church. With the longevity of his service as well as the vast network he has created through his work internationally, there are few, if any, more qualified to speak practical wisdom about raising a new generation for the Lord through cross-cultural ministry in general and Chinese churches in particular.

Shawn Isaacs
Youth Pastor
Cincinnati Chinese Church

I've been in student ministry for over 25 years. This is the time more than ever for us as the church to be agents of change, if we are truly going to reach this next generation with the gospel. Reggie Tsang not only has a heartfelt passion for students, he is extremely knowledgeable with practical ways on how to reach students with God's word. *Coffee with Uncle Reggie 3* shows the joy and passion a church should have to reach students for Christ. This book features tremendous stories that present ways to reach our youth today, and solid take-aways that churches can use to reach this next generation.

Stan Elder
National Team Strategist
National Network of Youth Ministries

In 1976, when I first came from Taiwan to Cincinnati to study, I joined the Cincinnati Chinese Church, where I met Elder Tsang. At that time, the church was just six years old. Under the leadership of Dr. Tsang, Bro. Shipei Chu and Dr. Louie, the three founding elders, the church was full of energy and spiritual power. Elder Tsang had come from Hong Kong and worked in the Cincinnati Children's Hospital. His career had just taken off and he was very busy. But thanks to his love for the Lord, his work never hindered his ministry in the church. He was responsible for the visitation in

不能的事，在上帝却能。曾振锚——或是用"曾叔叔"这个亲切的称谓——一生大部分时间都在看着上帝在辛城教会做那些在人看来是不可能的事。凭借他长期的服务以及他通过国际工作所建立的广泛网络，几乎没有人更有资格谈论怎样以切实的智慧，通过跨文化事工和华语教会为主培养新的一代。

肖恩·以撒斯
辛城教会青年事工牧师

我从事学生事工已经超过 25 年。如果我们真的要把福音传给下一代，现在正是教会作为变革推动者的最佳时候。曾振锚不仅对学生有发自内心的热情，他更非常了解如何切实地把上帝的话语带给学生。《兴起新一代服事》显示了教会为向学生传福音所必须具有的喜悦和激情。本书讲述了许多故事，这些故事提供了接触当今的青年人的办法，以及教会可以用来影响下一代的扎实的参考实例。

斯坦·爱德
美国青年事工网络团队策略师

1976 年，我从台湾到美国辛城大学念书时，加入了辛城教会，在那里认识了曾振锚长老。那时教会刚过六个年头，在曾医生、朱斯白弟兄和雷兆轸医生三位长老的带领之下，教会一片生气，充满灵力。从香港来的曾长老在辛辛那提儿童医院工作，事业刚刚起飞，忙的不得了。但是多亏他爱主的心，他的工作毫不耽误教会的服事。他负责探访的工作，每周六晚都把弟兄姊妹组成一个个的小队，去向人传福音。这不仅是一晚的活动，而是要花许多时间去联

church. Every Saturday night, he organized brothers and sisters to form into small teams to visit people and share the good news. This work was not a one-night event, but took a lot of time to contact, arrange the participants and the people to be visited, write the records and do follow-ups after the visit, and so on. Every Thursday night, he would call church brothers and sisters with just one sentence: "Are you going to visit on Saturday?" Some people were even afraid to answer the phone on Thursday night, but every time they came back from the visitation, they were full of joy, no matter what the results were. Simply in this service, he faithfully served for more than ten years. It is obvious that he is passionate for people's souls and we can tell how sincere he is at heart.

The establishment of the Cincinnati Chinese Church is based on foundational biblical principles. As mentioned in the chapter "Decisions, Decisions, Decisions II: Spirit to Consensus" in the book, the characteristic of the Cincinnati Chinese Church is that decision-making is guided by the Holy Spirit, and we believe that God will surely give a unified result for all. Therefore, there are no "minority submitting to majority" decisions in our church, and there is no anonymous voting. In everything we seek consensus approval. When the congregation increases, the church may use representatives to participate in decision-making or adopt a consensus approach. Elder Tsang had a strong belief in this principle and led the church to always walk on the path of unity.

There are many good examples set by Elder Tsang, which are very real and beautiful. After he retired from the first line of church governance, God gave him the gift of writing, and gradually he plans to express in words how God taught him to serve others, enabling more people to be followers in Jesus' footsteps. Now that he has moved away, we always feel a great loss; but in fact he did not leave, because his example is always engraved in our hearts.

David Wu
Senior Pastor
Cincinnati Chinese Church

系，安排参与探访的人、被探访的对象、探访后的记录和跟进等等。每到周四晚，他都会打电话给弟兄姊妹，只一句话：「周六去不去探访？」有些人甚至怕周四晚接电话，但每次参加探访，回来都是满心喜乐，不论成果如何。光是这一件服事，他就忠心地做了十余年，可见他热爱人灵魂得救的心，是何等的迫切真诚。

　　辛城教会的建立，是基于回到圣经的基础上。正如本书第14章"决定、决定、决定（二）：圣灵、合一"所提及，辛城教会的特色是，事情的决定是取决于圣灵的引导，我们相信上帝必然会使所有人都达到一致的结果。所以在辛城教会没有"少数服从多数"，也没有匿名投票这些人为的方法。每件事都是寻求全体一致通过。当教会人数增多时，会众可以用代表来参与决策，或是采取一致通过的方法。曾长老对此原则有很强的信念，也令教会始终走在合一的路上。

　　曾长老立下的榜样很多，很真，也很美。他从教会治理第一线上退下来后，上帝给他写作的恩赐，渐渐地他计画把上帝教导他怎样服事别人的方法用文字表达出来，能够使更多人跟随耶稣的脚踪。没有他在身边，我们总觉得是很大的失落；但其实他也没有离开，因为他的榜样始终铭刻在我们心上。

吴继扬
辛城教会资深牧师

翻译：Frank、Ira

Introduction

Uncle Reggie served for many decades in numerous capacities at the Cincinnati Chinese Church. That experience has given him a *practical* perspective about growing an ethnic church, and the special challenges of leadership in such a setting. His particular burden has always been the raising of the next generation of believers committed to serving the Lord; this burden is a major reason for this book.

Uncle Reggie was a founding elder of the Cincinnati Chinese Church in October, 1970, along with now-deceased Elders Shipei Chu and David Louie. Over the 46 years of Uncle Reggie's eldership, the church became a very active, outreach-conscious ethnic church of believers with origins from Taiwan, Hong Kong, China and USA, providing a complex multicultural backdrop to this book. Uncle Reggie is quintilingual, and his language skills likely helped in understanding and bridging the complex multilingual and multicultural challenges of an ethnic church.

Initially, in the first 14 years, Elder Reggie worked particularly in an executive minister role, with Elder Chu in the senior preaching minister role. During two periods when Elder Chu was transferred away from Cincinnati by his company, Reggie was left as the only functioning minister and main preacher. After full-time ministers joined the church, Elder Reggie, by now uniformly known by young and old as "Uncle Reggie," considered his main role was to complement and assist the leadership of the full-time ministers. However he continued to step in as substitute minister and preacher in gap periods, including the new English ministry, in its beginning and for periods between ministers. All in all, through the life of the church, he was essentially acting minister for seven times!

While serving as elder plus active physician-scientist for 24 years, and later as full-time elder and missionary for 22 years, for a total of 46 years,

引言

曾叔叔在辛城教会参与了各种服事几十年,这种经验令他对推动族群教会的发展,以及带领者在这样一个环境中面对什么特殊挑战等方面,都有*切实的*见解。一直以来,他在培养下一代忠心事主的信徒方面有特殊的负担,这是本书成书的主要原因。

1970 年 10 月,曾叔叔与现在已安息主怀的朱斯白和雷兆轸长老一起,成立了辛城教会。在曾叔叔担任长老的 46 年里,辛城教会成为一个非常活跃、外展意识强烈的族群教会,信徒来自台湾、香港、中国大陆和美国,这为本书提供了复杂多元的文化背景。曾叔叔懂得多种语言,他在语言技能方面的特长有助他理解和弥合族群教会中由于多种语言和文化不同而出现的问题。

在最初的 14 年里,曾长老主要侧重于教会行政方面的职责,朱长老则担任主任传道职务。当中有两个时期,朱长老被公司调职离开辛辛那提,留下曾叔叔作为唯一的行政管理者和主任传道。在全职教牧们加入教会后,教会中不论老幼都亲切地称曾长老为"曾叔叔"。从那时起,曾长老的主要角色变成了弥补和协助全职教牧的领导。但在牧师和传道人出缺期间,譬如在英文堂聚会刚起步时,或在英语传道职位来不及交接时,他仍然挺身而出,暂代这些职务。总而言之,在教会的生活中,他有七次实际上是在行使代理牧师之责!

在担任教会长老的 24 年中,曾叔叔还是个全职医生和科研工作者;后来,他又担任教会全职长老和传道人 22 年,合共 46 年。他享受带领会众,开拓并组织许多新的事工,譬如种子教会、教会

Uncle Reggie enjoyed taking the lead in many efforts. These included beginning and organizing numerous new ministries: the embryonic church, evangelism outreach, vacation bible school, youth ministry, missions, and English ministry. This gave him a unique perspective on the many and varied ministries. It was a great joy for him to watch as the church grew steadily from 20-30 members, eventually becoming a 500-member church of three congregations.

Uncle Reggie has always loved having one-on-one lunch or "coffee with Uncle Reggie" chats with many church and ministry leaders as well as youth, sometimes literally every day of the week, learning about practical issues from their personal lives and ministries, and telling them many relevant and encouraging stories from his abundant and varied life experiences.

In this book, he particularly weaves in such stories and principles, in his trademark "coffee with Uncle Reggie" style. In an easy "chatty" way, often with humor mixed in, he suggests how we might integrate key biblical principles into church ministries. His focus is particularly on the *practical* work of raising a new generation to serve, with the assumption that preaching and teaching topics are much better covered by numerous other available scholarly writings.

As senior elder, Uncle Reggie initiated a workshop series with the senior pastor for new deacon groups, to orientate them to their new responsibilities. While giving talks to the deacons, he soon realized that many of these principles were quite new to them. Or they were hidden somewhere in their past experiences in church, but had never been clarified or spelled out before. Many themes have flowed from these talks into this book, reflecting real-life issues of those serving the church in various ministries.

Uncle Reggie's most basic passion has clearly been the next generation, from childhood to youth to young adulthood, to mobilize "youth for all nations", a strong biblical concept. These ministry areas are normally particularly challenging, and more so especially for ethnic churches. Growing up in a multicultural and multilingual environment in Asia likely gave Uncle

中的传福音外展、暑期圣经班、青少年事工、宣道事工、英语事工等等。这一切经验使他对许多不同的事工都有独特的见解。当教会从 20 至 30 名成员稳步增长，成为由 500 人和 3 个聚会点组成的教会时，他大感欣慰。

曾叔叔一直喜欢一对一地与教会的年轻人、同工和事工负责人午餐，或是称为"与曾叔叔闲聊"的喝咖啡时间。有时候，甚至一周中的每一天他都会有约。在与他人沟通时，曾叔叔发现各人生活和事工中的实际问题，然后从他丰富多样的生活经历中，给他们讲许多相关的故事，鼓励他们。

在这本书中，他收集了许多这样的故事和主题，并以特有的"与曾叔叔闲聊"的风格记录下来。他以一种简单的"闲谈"方式，常常伴之以幽默的言语，展现给我们看如何将重要的圣经真理融入教会事工中。他特别将重点放在*切实*培养新一代服事主，因为他认为讲道和主日学专题已经由其他很多专著更好地涵盖了。

作为资深长老，曾叔叔与主任牧师一起为新上任的执事团发起了一系列的研讨会，以帮助他们理解新的职责。在给执事做培训时，他很快意识到许多原则对他们来说都是新的概念。或者那是他们过去在教会服事时，曾模模糊糊地感觉到但却从未清楚地认识到的。这些讲座的主题有许多都在本书中展示了，充分反映出教会服事中会出现的实际问题。

曾叔叔最大的感动显然是服事下一代，从少年到青年再到成年，动员"普世青少年"为上帝的国行动起来，这是圣经中反复强调的一个概念。这些事工领域通常特别具有挑战性，特别是对于族群教会而言，更是如此。在亚洲多元文化和多种语言的环境中长大的曾叔叔，他的成长经历赋予他一个特殊的视角；而他在新生儿医

Reggie some special perspective, while his academic passion in the field of neonatal pediatrics further strengthened his passion for strong foundational early life development.

So, this book is meant to be read easily, on a "one plane ride" basis, as a story-book series. And to be read again, as needed, supplemented by lots of Uncle Reggie stories on Reggietales.org. Life is a journey of many stories, and you are invited on this wonderful story and journey of serving the Lord, in many and interesting ways.

学领域中的学术热情则进一步加强了他呵护和培养灵里新生命的激情。

所以，这本书的初衷是作为"飞机上的简单阅读物"，属于轻松阅读的故事书系列。根据个人的需要，你可以反复阅读，并以在 Reggietales.org 上找到的许多曾叔叔的故事来补充。生活是由许多故事组成的旅程，我邀请你来体验这个服事主的美妙旅程，旅程中充满了惊喜。

翻译：孟瑄

Acknowledgements

I wish to thank especially Deacon Peter Yang, who has enthusiastically encouraged me to write my Uncle Reggie Stories, and particularly this book, which he felt might fill an important gap among Chinese churches. I have "grown up in" and visited many Asian churches in both North America and Asia, over many decades of life, and from these visits I have gathered a great deal of information about problems and issues that arise in efforts to start an Asian church. Especially the concerns about the next generation, which are particularly challenging to an ethnic church.

Serving over 46 years in the Cincinnati Chinese Church has been a wonderful experience of love and cooperative venture. Especially in the beginning years of building a living church, the vision and goals of starting a new (and only) Chinese church in Cincinnati, inspired an amazingly focused effort by all the co-workers. I can barely remember any real arguments, as we all had to work hard to start the church, and solve the numerous problems that arose. Here, I particularly express heartfelt deep appreciation for our co-founder of the church, now-deceased Elder Shipei Chu and his dedicated wife Elaine, who were truly selfless and passionate to serve God without fail, whose "walk the talk" life gave my wife and me much inspiration and encouragement.

Later generations of ministers and their spouses, especially senior Pastor David Wu, and his wife Rebecca, with their tireless dedication and commitment, helped complete my education and training in church leadership. It has truly been a joy to serve with wonderful pastors and ministers over the years: Simon Chen, K.C. Fang, Robert Altstadt, Mary Leung, Stan Elder, Eric Chang, Shawn Isaacs, and Bobby Yang. The "young" ministers' enthusiasm and careful thoughtfulness have continued to inspire and encourage me, so that I feel we have now happily handed over leadership

致谢

我要特别感谢杨华礼执事，他热情地鼓励我写下曾叔叔的故事，尤其是这本书，因为他觉得这本书可能填补了华人教会之中的重要空白。在几十年的生活中，我"成长于"并探访过北美及亚洲的不少亚洲教会。从这些经历中，我收集了一些与建立亚洲教会相关的资讯和实际面对的问题。尤其是对于下一代的事工，这个领域对于族群教会而言是特别具挑战性的。

在辛城教会服事的 46 年，是一段充满了爱和默契的美好历程。特别是在建立一个有活力的教会的最初几年中，在辛辛那提建立一个新的、也是唯一的华语教会的愿景和目标激发了所有同工为了一个共同目标而专注努力。我几乎想不起我们发生过任何真正的争执，因为我们都在努力地建立教会，解决所面临的众多问题。在这里，我特别衷心感谢我们教会的联合创始人，现已去世的朱斯白长老，和他忠实的妻子刘依南。朱长老夫妇真诚、无私、热心地服事上帝，他们的"言传身教"，在生活中给我和我的妻子很多激励和鼓舞。

后来的牧师，特别是资深牧师吴继扬和他的妻子赵嘉昕，以不懈的奉献和忠诚的精神，帮助我完成了在教会领导方面的教育和培训。多年来，与陈思宁、方冠杰、罗伯特·阿尔斯塔特、梁坤仪、斯坦·爱德、张凯哲、肖恩·以撒斯和杨洋等牧师及传道人一起服事，令我充满了喜乐。"年轻"牧者的热情和细心体贴将继续激励和鼓舞我。因此，我觉得我们现在已经欣然将领导权交给了大有潜力和希望的新一代。

to a new generation with great potential and promise.

It is my dream and concern that I could help cover specific church leadership issues in a positive way, that could be helpful for the church in one of its primary missions, to raise a new generation to faithfully serve God. I feel deeply that He has given Asian churches a special opportunity and privilege to serve Him, and we should try to maximize what we can do in His Name and for His Glory!

Uncle Reggie
Newcastle Brookside
Greater Seattle, Washington, USA

我的梦想和目标是，我能以正面的方式协助处理有关教会领导的具体问题，这对教会的其中一个主要任务，即培养新一代忠心地服事上帝，可能会有帮助。我深深地感到，祂给了亚洲教会一个特别的机会和特权来事奉祂，我们应该尽力奉祂的名行事，荣耀祂！

曾叔叔
美国华盛顿州大西雅图地区
纽卡斯尔市"溪水河畔"

翻译：孟瑄

1. Children's Ministry is Our Foundational Treasure

In all my professional life I have been working with small babies, literally from the moment of their birth, and even while they are still in the mother's womb! Everything around these babies can affect them, from stimulation to their senses, to oxygen levels, to nutrition, to a host of other influences. Some brief influences can even have long-term impact, sometimes for life. We talk about how, at certain times in our lives, "minutes count": this is one of those times. One could even say, "Sometimes, seconds count!" The very early phases in life are truly critically important; hence my many decades of research, papers and grants, focused around this phase of life, while I was providing intensive care for these infants when they were sick.

D.L. Moody of Chicago had a keen sense of the critical importance of childhood influences. He went around his neighborhood and literally grabbed and herded children into his Sunday Schools, to hear the word of God. These kids were highly vulnerable to the dangers and temptations of the big city, but he taught them well, bringing up many of them as responsible citizens. They became the beginning of his church congregation, which grew and grew. Moody ultimately ministered to tens of thousands of people, and started Moody Bible Institute, which has sent tens of thousands of young ministers and missionaries all over the world. In turn, many of these missionaries, recognizing acutely the importance of children's work, began their ministries with a strong emphasis on children, an excellent model that is effective in diverse cultures and lands.

In Hong Kong, my wife (to be) and I grew up in the Swatow Christian Church, a strong evangelical church with an effective Sunday School program

1. 儿童事工是我们的宝贵根基

在我整个职业生涯中，我一直与小婴儿一起工作，不只从他们出生那一刻开始，甚至追溯到他们还在母亲子宫里的时候！这些婴儿周围的一切都可以影响他们，从刺激他们的感官，到氧气水平、营养，以至其他一系列影响。许多短暂的影响，可能会造成长期的问题，甚至会影响他们的一生。我们谈论到对生命的某些阶段来说，时间是如何重要，甚至达到"分秒必争"的程度，而婴儿期就是这样的一个时期。生命的早期阶段确实非常重要，因此我几十年的研究、论文和研究经费，都集中在这个生命阶段，同时我又为生病的婴儿提供重症照护。

芝加哥的穆迪敏锐地意识到童年影响的重要性。他绕着自己的街区，把路上的孩子们带入主日学校，让他们学习上帝的话。这些在路上遊荡的孩子极易受到大城市的危害和诱惑，但穆迪把他们教得很好，让他们长大后成为负责任的公民，也借此开始了他教会的聚会，教会也逐渐增长和发展。穆迪最终牧养了数万人，并创立了穆迪圣经学院，该学院已派遣了数万名年轻的传道人和宣道士到世界各地。这些宣道士有许多都察觉到儿童工作的重要性，因此非常强调儿童事工，而这种优秀的模式在不同文化和地方都很有效。

在香港，我和我的妻子（当时我们还未成婚）在潮人生命堂长大，这是一个颇有规模的福音派教会，为儿童和青少年提供有效的

for children and youth. We even became "childhood sweethearts" under the nurture and, I sometimes suspect, the blessing (!) of excellent Sunday School teachers, whom I remember vividly and fondly, even to their old age. One of my most admired teachers, Charles, lived to the very ripe age of 90, and yet was still able to quote his childhood memorized Bible verses, even when he had dementia in his final years.

Our Sunday School teachers were undoubtedly great role models who had tremendous impact on our young lives. Even as the church children grew up and migrated to Australia and America, we could see the impact of their childhood Sunday School. Many continued to serve the Lord, and became deacons, elders, ministers and leaders of their churches. We heard enough stories from all over the world to remind us that, even when it seemed that some had veered from the straight and narrow, later on we heard, to our great encouragement, that many had returned to church to serve faithfully.

Al grew up as a child in the church, but when he left high school, he moved overseas. He became extremely successful and well-off in his new country, and drifted away from church. He spent every weekend basically playing mahjong with his friends, with little meaningful purpose in life. One weekend he was doing the same, but as he drove home, he noticed his two precious daughters sleeping in the back seat,

敬畏主的主日学教师侯老师与他美好的家庭。他活到 90 岁，一生致力于教育。多年来，他是我和我妻子的活榜样。

God-fearing dedicated Sunday School teacher, Charles, shown with his lovely family. He lived until he was 90 years old, faithfully teaching all his life. A living, walking role model for my future wife and me, for years.

主日学课程。我和我太太在主日学老师的培育下成了"青梅竹马"的恋人，我有时更怀疑，这是归功于主日学老师们的祝福（！）。我对这些老师仍然有鲜明和亲切的印象，他们即使到了晚年，都是优秀的主日学老师。活到 90 岁高龄的侯老师是我最敬仰的其中一位老师，即使他在最后几年患有认知障碍症，但仍能引用他儿时背诵的圣经经文。

我们的主日学老师无疑是伟大的榜样，对我们年幼的生活产生了巨大的影响。即使教会中的孩子长大了，并迁居澳洲和美国，我们也能在他们身上看到童年时期主日学的影响。其中许多人继续事奉主，成为他们教会的执事、长老、传道人和领袖。我们听到来自世界各地的故事，它们都提醒我们，即使看起来有些人曾经偏离了正路、窄路，但后来我们都听说，许多人回到教会忠心地事奉，这给我们极大的鼓舞。

阿尔在教会里长大，但高中毕业后就搬到海外。他在新的国家变得非常成功和富裕，并远离了教会生活。他每个周末都和朋友一起打麻将，生活中没什么目标。一个周末他同样去了打麻将，但当他开车回家时，他注意到他们的两个宝贝女儿在后座睡觉，因为他和妻子拖着她们一起度过他们平时的麻将之夜。

当时已经过了午夜，他转向妻子说："我们怎会这样对待孩子？我们正过着怎样的人生？也许我们应该返回教会。"他的妻子也同意，于是二人毅然退出原来的麻将四人组，"回到"教会，不久之后就开始事奉主了。在我看来，毫无疑问，他童年时期的主日学已经永远影响了他的生活，即使是在遥远异地的生活。他忠心的母亲自他小时候就每天为他所作的祈祷，终于也得到了回应。

现今有许多非常好的书籍可以帮助我们从事儿童事工，所以没

because he and his wife had dragged them along for their usual mahjong night.

As this was way past midnight, he turned to his wife and said, "What are we doing with our children? What kind of life are we leading? Maybe we should go back to church." His wife agreed to this, and they abruptly withdrew from their mahjong "4-legged" group, "returned" to church, and after a while began to serve the Lord. In my view, there was little question that his childhood Sunday School had impacted his life forever, even in a far-away foreign place. And that his faithful mother's daily prayer for him from childhood had finally been answered.

When we work in children's ministries today, there are lots of very fine books to help us, so there is no need to repeat what they say. I would just like to emphasize that children's ministry is so important that it definitely needs *a big team effort*, requiring a lot of people working together, joyfully, with one great goal. Never attempt to do this with only a few people, or everyone will burn out quickly and fail. Find good people, inspire them, gather them together, pray together for the kids, and off we go. We can all learn and grow together.

Most people, probably especially Asians from overseas, are hesitant to volunteer themselves for most church work, from a combination of shyness, humility, and inertia, so don't wait for them to volunteer. Just help "volunteer them," with a smile and warmth. If they are scared at first, especially about language issues with American-born children, they can come in as observers and assistants. They can also help first in Vacation Bible School work, which is an excellent training ground; see chapter 2: "*Lord, Bring us 100 Children.*" Teenage volunteers especially will likely be inspired by Vacation Bible School; keep encouraging them to join as fresh Sunday School teacher assistants, and watch them grow into great teachers.

A key to the work of Sunday School is to find a credible experienced person as *recruiter and mobilizer*, one who obviously loves children, who is willing to announce, announce, announce, at big and small meetings, about

有必要重复他们所说的话。我只想强调，儿童事工是如此重要，绝对需要*庞大团队的努力*，需要很多人一起和谐快乐地工作，共同迈向一个伟大的目标。儿童事工无论何时都不应该只由少数人来做，否则很快就会精疲力尽并且失败。寻找出色的人，激励他们，把他们聚集起来，一起为孩子祷告，然后开始同工。我们都可以一起学习和成长。

大多数人，或许尤其是来自海外的亚洲人，都会在羞怯、谦卑和被动的共同作用下，迟疑不肯自荐参与教会的大部分工作。所以，不要等他们自愿，要用微笑和亲切的态度"帮助他们成为志愿者"。如果他们害怕，特别是与美国出生的孩子在语言沟通上有问题，他们仍然可以作为助手，或在一旁观察。他们也可以先在假期圣经班中帮忙，这是一个很好的训练场（参阅本书第 2 章："*主啊，给我们 100 个孩子*"）。十来岁的志愿者尤其可能受到假期圣经班的启发；所以我们要继续鼓励他们加入主日学成为教师助理，并见证他们成长，成为优秀的老师。

主日学事工的一项要诀，是找到一位可靠而有经验的人，作为*招聘人员和动员者*，这人显然爱孩子，愿意用热情和灿烂的笑容，在大大小小的会议上宣布再宣布，宣布儿童事工的需求、挑战以及成果。大多数教会的会众几乎未曾注意过儿童事工，往往是"眼不见，心不烦"，所以我们有责任让儿童事工项目保持活力，让其他教会成员在意这项事工。

主日学一项很重要的任务，是教导孩子*直觉性*的习惯和原则。虽然我们总会开玩笑说，"所有问题的正确回答一定是耶稣"，但这却是千真万确的。我们的目标是培养年轻人的直觉，以致他们在生命中的*任何时刻*、任何地点都能做正确的事。在这个邪恶和不断

the needs, challenges and results of the children's programs, with enthusiasm and a great smile! Most church congregations barely see the children's program, being often "out of sight, out of mind", so it is up to us to keep the program alive and well in the minds of the adults.

One of the most important things that happens in Sunday School is teaching children great *instinctive* habits and principles, where indeed "the answer is always Jesus," as we like to joke about, but is true. Our goal is to nurture instincts in young people to do the right thing *all the time*. And everywhere in their lives. In this evil and deteriorating world, when faced with temptations and wrongdoing, hesitation can be lethal. I am not kidding or joking: the reported suicides, drug overdoses, and shootings often occur around faulty instinctive decision making. And wrong, impetuous small decisions, at many forks of road, can lead unwittingly down terrible pathways. Principles and discipline are undoubtedly best taught in childhood, as foundational solid bases for their whole lives.

For example, even simple habits of discipline can have valuable long-term impact. Teaching children to *tithe* regularly from childhood, even with small amounts, gives children a foundation of the right attitude and discipline towards God, giving, and serving others for a lifetime. That was how my wife and I were taught faithfully as children, and it was *instinctive* for us all our lives; therefore as adults, we had little hesitation over giving in diverse situations, even when we were quite poor, such as during our pediatric training years. Amazingly, God has blessed us abundantly, throughout our entire lives, in unexpected and joyful ways, much more than we deserve, just like we were taught in Sunday School.

A story* goes that the tireless servant of God, George Mueller, was asked one time how many people accepted the Lord, after a meeting at which he had been speaking. When he responded, "two and a half people," people assumed he meant that there were two adults and one child. But he meant two children and one adult. Why? He explained that the two children still had most of their lives to live, and the adult had only half a life left! An important

恶化的世界中面对诱惑和不法行为时，只要稍为犹豫，都有可能致命。我不是在开玩笑或说笑：自杀、药物滥用和枪击事件，往往是环绕错误的直觉性决定而出现。在有多个岔路的路口，任何错误而冲动的小决定，都会无意识地导向一条可怕的道路。毫无疑问，原则和纪律最好是在儿童时期教导，成为他们一生坚固的基础。

例如，即使是简单的纪律习惯也会产生宝贵的长期影响。教导儿童从童年起就定期*十一奉献*，即使是少量的金钱，也可以为儿童奠定一生的基础，终生以正确的态度和纪律对待上帝、奉献和服务他人。这就是我和妻子小时候一直接受的教导方式，也成为我们一生的*本能*。因此，成年后，即使在我们很困乏的时候，例如在儿科训练期间，我们也毫不犹豫地给予各种帮助。令人惊讶的是，就像我们在主日学中所受的教导那样，上帝在我们的一生中，总以喜出望外的方式给我们丰富的福气，远远超出了我们应得的。

有个故事＊是这样的：为上帝勤奋不懈地工作的乔治·穆勒，在一次他负责讲道的聚会后被问及有多少人接受了上帝。他回答"两个半人"，人们认为他的意思是有两个成年人和一个孩子。但其实他的意思是两个孩子和一个成人。为什么？他解释说，这两个孩子还有一辈子要过，而成年人只剩半辈子！这个故事的一个重要推论是，*儿童主日学绝对是为终生而不仅仅是半生作准备*。

总的来说，主日学这类事工最令人惊讶的是，对于孩子们而言，有*真实*的榜样在他们眼前与他们互动，爱他们和启发他们。这些都不是电视、视频或智能手机里的人物。这些教师通常都不是由大学教授培训的"专业老师"，而是真实生活中同样会犯错的教练，像孩子的亲生父母和兄姊一样，充满爱心，年复一年，特别对孩子们的灵命成长作出贡献。

corollary to this story is that *children's* Sunday School is definitely a great preparation for all of life, not just a half.

Overall, the astonishing thing about programs like Sunday School is that, for the children, right before their eyes, there are *walking* role models interacting with them, loving and inspiring them. These are not TV, video or smartphone characters. These are usually not "professional teachers", taught and trained by college professors, but real-life fallible coaches, just like natural parents and older siblings to the Sunday School kids, committed specifically and lovingly to their spiritual growth, for years and years.

Growing up in such an atmosphere of love and mission, kids instinctively carry that message all their lives. I am always thankful for the generations of wonderful dedicated Sunday School teachers who inspired us as children, so that we ourselves *in turn* can become dedicated Sunday School teachers. As they say, "life lessons are best *caught*, than *taught*," and that is where Sunday School teachers are so wonderful. I personally feel that Sunday School teaching ranks as the "best job" in life; we can, literally, nurture and inspire numerous others in life, naturally, and with the greatest satisfaction.

Finally, exposure to different ministry opportunities can begin really young. For my wife and me, even though we grew up as preteens in different countries, separated by a thousand miles, both sets of our parents used to entertain foreign missionaries in our homes. From these gatherings, we learned from early childhood the importance of missions work, which helped set the stage for a lifetime of meaningful commitment to serving in missions. So much so that we willingly and joyfully left a very promising academic career to serve in medical missions in China. A perfect decision in time and place, linked clearly to childhood training and discipline. I invite you to read my book, *Coffee with Uncle Reggie*; you will see how joyful my life became, as I stepped into the "mission world." A strong foundation in childhood is truly a treasure.

Author's caveat: I can't actually find this exact reference anymore, so if you find it, please let me know. It's a great story anyway, with strong implications.

1. 儿童事工是我们的宝贵根基
1. Children's Ministry is Our Foundational Treasure

在这种充满爱与使命的氛围中成长的孩子，将会终其一生按着直觉带着这样的价值观走下去。对一代又一代敬业的主日学老师，我一直心存感激，这些老师启发了儿时的我们，叫我们自己*继而*也可以成为敬业的主日学老师。俗语说："最好的人生功课是*领悟*得来的，而不是*被教*出来的。"这就是主日学老师的美好之处。我个人认为，主日学的教学是人生中"最好的工作"，我们可以自然地并以最大的满足感，来培养和启发生活中其他众多的人。

最后，我们可以很年轻就开始接触不同的事奉机会。对于我和我的妻子来说，尽管我们十多岁之前是在不同国家成长，相距千里之外，但我们两家的父母都曾经在家中招待外国宣道士。这些聚会让我们在幼儿时期就了解宣道工作的重要性，这为终身服事的奉献精神奠定了基础。影响如此之深，以致我们愿意欣然离开了非常有前途的学术生涯，去中国从事医疗事工。这个在时间和地点方面都完美的决定，显然与童年的训练和教养相关。我邀请你阅读我的书《与曾叔叔闲聊》，你将看到我步入"宣道世界"后的生活变得多么喜乐。儿童时期建立的坚固基础的确是一个珍宝。

＊笔者的说明：我已经无法找到这个故事的准确来源，如果你找到它，请告诉我。这是一个伟大的故事，寓意深刻。

翻译：庄文菁

营会中的儿童和青年。营会意味着远离日常的学校生活和环境一段时间，是一个专注于上帝的时间，一个让老师与孩子增进关系的时间，此时的老师为孩子树立鲜活的榜样。我和妻子粹英一生都热爱儿童和青少年的退修会。

Children and youth at camp. Camp implies a time away from normal school routine and environment, a time to focus on God, a time for teachers to bond with their children, to be even more a walking role model for them. Esther and I have loved children and youth retreats, all of our lives.

2. Lord, Give Us 100 Children

In January, 1981, the brothers and sisters of the Cincinnati Chinese Church felt God's burden on their hearts to have a Vacation Bible School of our own. Many years ago we had helped our Caucasian brothers and sisters in their Vacation Bible Schools, but over the years, this interest and involvement had dwindled. "Start our own Vacation Bible School?" "Who's going to volunteer?" "Who's willing to take off from work to help?" Thus said, I took a straw poll of twenty or so "workers" at our monthly workers' meeting. To my surprise, a dozen hands shot up. "I take it you're serious!" So we began praying, praying that God would indeed give us the wisdom and love for the task. We bought a series of "VBS" materials, invited an experienced VBS leader to speak to us, prayed for teachers, asked for volunteers to be drivers, and on and on it went. It was just amazing to see how God opened door after door. There was the entire Church working together, praying together, planning together, and we could feel the excitement in the air.

We prayed for 40 children, double the size of our Sunday School classes. We started to make phone calls. One sister invited seven or eight families. "Would you like to have your children come to Vacation Bible School?" "How much will it cost?" "Nothing! And we will pick up your children and return them to your home!" "Oh, that's too much of a burden for you: bu hao yi si." "We want to share God's love with your children and with you!" And two weeks before the VBS opening date, God had already given us 40 children. We were overjoyed! "We should pray for more – let's pray for 60!" Unbelievably (if one is permitted to use such a word), more than 60 children came to VBS!

2. 主啊，给我们 100 个孩子

1981 年 1 月，辛城教会的弟兄姐妹们感到上帝放在他们心里的负担，要创办我们自己的儿童暑期圣经班。很多年前，我们在白人弟兄姐妹举办的暑期圣经班中帮过忙。但是这么多年过去后，参与的兴趣逐渐降低了。"我们自己开办暑期圣经班吗？""谁会自愿参与呢？""谁愿意请假来帮忙呢？"于是，我在每月同工会上对约 20 位"同工"做了个非正式的民意调查。很意外，有 12 双手举起来了。"我就当你们是认真的！"所以我们就开始祷告，祈求上帝在这件事工上赐我们智慧和爱心。我们买了一套暑期圣经班教材，邀请了有经验的暑期圣经班带领者给我们讲课，为我们的老师祷告，物色志愿者作驾驶员等等。看到上帝是如何把一扇又一扇门打开，实在是很奇妙的事。那时，整个教会都同心协力地工作，一起祷告，一起计画，我们能感到空气中那种兴奋的气息。

我们为 40 个孩子祷告，那是我们主日学人数的两倍。然后我们就开始打电话。一位姐妹邀请了七八个家庭。"你愿意让你的孩子来参加暑期圣经班吗？""多少钱？""不

早期在北丘教会举行的暑假圣经班，那里是我们教会早期的所在地。

Early days for VBS at Northern Hills Chapel, the early location of the church.

32 helpers called, drove, smiled, comforted, laughed and had some of the most meaningful moments of their lives. Snack time staffed by a group of mothers, game times led by the teenagers, crafts times assisted by a team of workers, singing time mixed with "Buzzy Bee", a fictionalized puppet show, and bible lessons plus a tension-packed missionary story kept the pace moving rapidly through the day.

Children are just lovely to watch. Day one, everyone was quiet and well behaved. Day two, they began to "learn the system"; not very quiet. Day three, they were ready to accept the Lord. Day four, they wanted to come back to Sunday School. Day five, all were excited about their evening performance, hoping their parents would come to their "graduation ceremony", and singing their hearts out, shouting their heads off in response to the puppets – "hello Buzzy Beeeee". The lovely smiles and warm hearts melted even unemotional Chinese hearts. It was a taste of heaven itself!

February, 1982: "Do we dare ask for more children this year?" "Lord, could we have a hundred children?" It was indeed an "unbelievable" number. An 80% increase. We would need 25 cars and more workers. Several key workers were in the middle of praying about moving out of town. Were we too "ambitious"? But again and again that number recurred. We prayed, but only "half-believing". Two weeks before the VBS only 60 children had registered. Had we asked for the wrong number? We kept praying. The day before VBS, 101 children had registered! The announcement brought tears to our eyes. God is indeed so good!

"The fields are indeed ripe unto harvest." There were so many families whom we could never reach before, who refused to even come close to a church, who now gladly let us take their children to church, who let them stay at times the entire Sunday afternoon at Church, who even let the children come to "Friday School" ("Sunday" School on Friday night). The children brought home their Bibles, their memory verses, their prayers, and what they learned at Sunday School. "Mom, don't be so sad, you can pray to God, He'll help you", is a recurring testimony of many mothers. And they have invited

用钱！而且我们还会来你家接送你的孩子。""噢，那太麻烦你了！不好意思。""我们想与你和你的孩子分享上帝的爱！"暑期圣经班开课日前的两个星期，上帝已为我们预备了 40 个孩子。我们太高兴了！"我们应该祷告要更多的孩子——让我们祷告求 60 个孩子吧！"难以相信（容我使用这个词），60 多个孩子来了暑期圣经班！

32 位同工打电话、开车、微笑、安慰、欢笑，过了一些他们一生中最有意义的时刻。点心时间由一群妈妈负责，游戏时间由青少年队带领，手工时间由同工队协助，唱歌时间掺了"嗡嗡蜜蜂"故事的木偶表演，还有圣经课加上一连串紧凑的宣道故事，使一天过得好快。

看着孩子们，就觉得他们实在很可爱。第一天，每个孩子都很安静很乖。第二天，他们开始"学懂了"，不太安静。第三天，他们已经准备好要接受耶稣为他们的救主了。第四天，他们想再来上主日学课。第五天，他们都为自己晚上的演出而十分兴奋，希望父母可以来参加他们的"毕业典礼"。他们尽情唱歌，大声地回应木偶："你好，嗡嗡蜜蜂"。可爱的笑脸和热烈的心甚至融化了不惯显露感情的成年华人的心。这是尝到天堂的滋味！

1982 年 2 月，我们问："我们今年还敢求更多的孩子吗？""主，我们可以有 100 个孩子吗？"这实在是一个"难以相信"的数目。增加了 80%。这样我们就需要 25 辆车和更多的同工。其中有好几位主力同工正在为是否要搬出城外而祷告。我们"雄心"太大了吗？但是一次又一次地，这个数字出现了。我们祷告了，但还是"半信半疑"。到了暑期圣经班开学前的两个星期，只有 60 个孩子报了名。我们所求的数目太大了吗？我们一直祷告。到了暑期圣经班开学前一天，有 101 个孩子报了名！这个宣布令我们涌出泪水。上帝实在是太好了！

their friends to come to Church. When we drop the children off at their doorsteps, many parents will welcome us into their homes and allow us an opportunity to share a moment of God's word with them. The doors that had been shut for years and years miraculously opened. Why didn't we do this earlier? Why did we waste all those years? Why didn't we believe our Lord when He said, "Forbid not the little children from coming to me. For such is the kingdom of Heaven."?

Closing ceremony VBS 1982. Ten classes "graduating" songs, puppet shows, bible verses, prizes. A twelve-year-old girl shared her lovely testimony, "At first I was scared to come up, but since the Lord wanted me to give a testimony I want to do so. When I came here to VBS last year, on the first day the Holy Spirit touched my heart, when I heard all the wonderful stories of Jesus, I accepted the Lord as my personal savior. I thank God for loving us so much. My little brother and I are grateful that the big church family accepted us as family members." Tears of joy mixed with songs of joy.

As we look to the years ahead, we pray for God's continued encouragement to us to look to the fields – the vast numbers of children that have ready, receptive hearts for the Lord, which will keep God's love and presence in their hearts, who will serve Him to the ends of the earth. May

that vision touch the hearts and minds of all Christians all over this land, to reach out and bring those lovely children into the Lord's presence! The joy and the challenge are before us!

后期在健康山主堂举行的暑假圣经班，可见我们需要很多志愿工作者。

Later days for VBS at our base church location on Compton shows the need for lots of volunteer staff.

2. 主啊，给我们 100 个孩子
2. Lord, Give Us 100 Children

"庄稼已经熟了，可以收割了。"有很多家庭我们以前从未接触过。他们甚至拒绝接近教会，但现在他们很乐意让我们把他们的孩子带来教会，有时让孩子们整个周日下午都留在教会，甚至让他们的孩子来"周五学校"（在周五晚上上课的"主日"学）。孩子们把他们的圣经、要背诵的金句、祷告和在主日学学到的东西都带回家。"妈妈，不要难过，你可以向上帝祷告，祂会帮助你"——这是很多妈妈的见证。他们又邀请了自己的朋友来教会。当我们把孩子送回家，来到家门口时，很多家长都会邀请我们进他们的家，让我们有机会与他们分享上帝的话。这些关闭了很多年的门奇迹般地开了。为什么我们不早点儿做呢？为什么这么多年来我们浪费了这么多时间呢？当我们的主说："让小孩子到我这里来，不要禁止他们；因为在天国的，正是这样的人"，为什么我们不相信祂？

在 1982 年暑期圣经班的结业礼上，有十班学生唱"毕业"歌，有木偶表演、圣经金句背诵和颁发奖项。一个 12 岁的女孩分享了她美好的见证："一开始，我怕上台，但是因为上帝要我做见证，我就想这样做。去年我来上暑期圣经班的第一天，圣灵感动了我。我听到这么多有关耶稣的动人故事后，就接受了主耶稣作为我的救主。我感谢上帝如此地爱我们。我和弟弟都很感激教会接受我们成为这个大家庭的成员。"喜悦的眼泪夹杂在喜乐的歌声中。

当我们展望未来，我们祷告求上帝继续鼓励我们举目向田观看——那儿有那么多孩子已经有了愿意接受上帝的心，他们会把上帝的爱放在他们的心中，他们将事奉祂直到地极。愿这个意象感动地上所有基督徒的心思意念，向可爱的孩子们伸出手，把他们带到上帝的国度里！这个喜乐和挑战就在我们面前！

翻译：Amy Zhao

3. Organizing a Strong Youth Program I: Youth for All Nations

I. Beginning an ethnic church children and youth program

My wife (to be) and I grew up in the Swatow Christian Church in Hong Kong, an excellent evangelical church with a great emphasis on children and youth programs. It was also an unusual ethnic church in that it used the Chaozhou or Swatow language exclusively, in a predominantly Cantonese city. We personally experienced the wonderful long-term impact of its many ministries, especially its strong emphasis on children and youth, throughout our own lives. So, when we helped start the Cincinnati Chinese Church fifty years ago, one of the first things we did was to help develop a solid children's program, and then soon thereafter the youth ministry.

Recognizing that children growing up in America are more American than Chinese, we emphasized the need for strong *English*-speaking teachers. Some people wanted to maintain Chinese culture and language through the Chinese church. However, we knew instinctively that

香港潮人生命堂青年团契的一个小组。我们就是在这个小组中成长，学会儿童和青年事工的重要性。
One small group of the youth program of the Swatow Christian Church in Hong Kong, where we grew up and learned how important the children and youth program was.

3. 组织强大的青年事工（一）：万国青年

1. 在族群教会展开儿童和青年事工

我和我的妻子（当时尚未结婚）在香港的潮人生命堂长大，那是一间出色的福音派教会，非常重视儿童和青年事工。它也是一座不寻常的族群教会，在一个以粤语为主的城市仅使用潮州话或汕头话。教会里面不同的事工，特别是对儿童和青年的重视，对我们的一生产生了很棒的长期影响。因此，50 年前，当我们帮忙建立辛城教会时，我们首先去做的其中一件事就是参与制定坚实的儿童事工计画，然后很快开展了青年事工。

我们认识到在美国长大的孩子更像美国人而不是中国人，因此需要有讲*英文*的好老师。有些人想通过华人教会保持中国文化和语言。但是，我们本能地知道讲英文的老师会更能帮助孩子们理解圣经和耶稣的教导。即使是不在美国出生，而与父母一起移民到美国的孩子，也很快会以说英语为主，只会在家中使用一些母语中的简单短语。当时，他们的母语可能是广东话、台湾话或后来的福州话，这些都与普通话完全不同。因此，如果在教堂里用中文教导孩子，实际上这通常意味着所用的是普通话。这对孩子们来说，很可能是第三种语言，会带来另一个麻烦。

English-speaking teachers would be better able to help kids understand the bible and Jesus' teachings. Even children who were not born in the USA but migrated with their parents to America quickly become predominantly English-speaking, except for simple phrases in the home language. And in those days, that language could be Cantonese, Taiwanese or, later, Fuzhounese, quite different from Mandarin altogether. So if the kids were taught in Chinese at church, in practice that would often mean Mandarin, a third language to them, creating yet another complication.

I remember visiting a Chinese church in Paris, where children and youth were expected to attend Sunday School *in Chinese* (I don't even remember which Chinese language), in order to maintain their Chinese proficiency. As a result, the children's and youth programs collapsed, apparently because the kids could not fully understand biblical concepts in Chinese, got bored with church, and dropped out one by one.

We really cannot easily mix the two underlying issues of language learning and faith: if we want to teach Chinese, a very good intention, we could and should do that as a distinct activity, in order to allow the teaching of the Bible and Christian principles in the most familiar tongue, which in our case, for American-born or -raised kids, would be English. The *primary* role of the ethnic church is still to teach the bible, not the ethnic culture or language. Ethnic churches that mixed their motives had mixed results. However, determined families that wanted to train their children in bicultural biblical literacy were able to do that at home, for example, by doing home bible readings in Chinese, which I think is an excellent approach.

2. Cooperation with other churches

At this juncture, God sent a faithful servant, Bruce, whom we met in the "American" church we used for our services in the first years. We became great friends, and Bruce would thereafter always pop up to help us when needed. Typically, he would volunteer for one-year commitments each time

我记得去过巴黎的一家华人教会，那里的儿童和青年要*用中文*来上主日学（我甚至不记得是中文的哪种方言），以保持他们的中文水准。结果，儿童和青少年事工失败了。这很明显是因为孩子们不能完全用中文理解圣经的概念，对教会生活感到无聊，然后一个接一个地离开。

我们不能轻易地将语言学习和信仰的两个基本问题混合在一起：如果我们想教中文（这当然是好事情），我们可以并且应该单独来教。而教导圣经和基督信仰的原则就应该用孩子们最熟悉的语言。对于美国出生或长大的孩子，最熟悉的语言是英语。族群教会的*主要*作用依然是教导圣经，而不是族群的文化或语言。有些族群教会混合了这两个动机，也就有了不一致的结果。但是，想要在双文化背景下对孩子进行圣经教导的家庭，可以在家中做到这一点，例如，在家中用中文阅读圣经，我觉得就是一种极好的方法。

2. 与其他教会合作

在我们主日去的"美国"教会的最初几年中，我们遇到了上帝派遣的忠心仆人布鲁斯，并且成为了很好的朋友。此后，布鲁斯总会在我们需要帮助时出现。通常，每次我们需要他时，他都会承诺为我们担当一年的志愿工作者。因为他认为经过一年后，我们将会建立了稳定的基础。这是一个极好的策略，使我们不必太依赖他，直接面对我们自己的问题！对了，布鲁斯实际上是白人，但他和我们如此亲切，使我们很容易忘记这一点。

更好的是，布鲁斯事后会继续推荐优秀的（也是白人的）志愿者给我们，尤其是来帮助我们的青年事工。这些志愿者通常都是年

we needed him, assuming that after that, we would be on a stable footing. That was an excellent strategy, which allowed us to not be too reliant on him and to face up to our own problems! Before I forget, Bruce is actually Caucasian, but it seemed so "natural" that it was easy to forget.

But the good thing was also that Bruce would later keep referring great (Caucasian) volunteers to us, especially to help our youth program, usually young men and women with a strong commitment to serve and willing to adapt to a cross-cultural situation. He himself would be available to be a special speaker, advisor or teacher as needed. He was essentially in many respects an "unofficial" *cofounder* of our church, from the critical beginning years, as well as at critical times later.

When we took youth teams to Central America to help the Chinese churches there, we discovered a commonplace phenomenon that illustrated the lessons and strengths of inter-church cooperation. There might be three Chinese churches in a city, all speaking different ethnic Chinese languages, coming from different cultural backgrounds (commonly Hong Kong, Mandarin-speaking from Taiwan, and Taiwanese). Because the adults were separated by language and culture, their youth groups were also kept separate, even though in reality they spoke one common language, i.e., *Spanish*. As the visiting mission team, we sensed the youth were, unfortunately, being kept separate mainly because of adult cultural differences, causing side effects on the youth and the youth programs. At least, that's how it seemed to us, as outsiders.

But whenever our Cincinnati mission team arrived on the scene, the local leaders would graciously allow their youth from all three churches to join in our activities together. This made for an excellent "critical mass effect", producing heartwarming youth activities, readily conducted in English and Spanish. Often we had a combined youth retreat, which was indeed very encouraging and inspirational for all, us included.

But the sad thing was that when we left, they broke back into three separate groups, each youth group too small to be effective, maybe only a

轻的男女，有委身事奉的决心，并愿意适应跨文化的环境。根据需要，布鲁斯本人会担任特别讲者、顾问或导师。从我们教会初创的头几年到后来的各个关键时刻，基本上他在许多方面都是我们教会的"非正式"*联合创办人*。

辛辛那提儿童和青年事工的初期：我们可以将所有儿童和青少年聚集在一个房间里。从小处开始，但要不断成长。

Beginning the program in Cincinnati: we could pack all the children and youth in one room. Start small but keep growing them.

当我们带青年队去中美洲帮助那里的华人教会时，我们发现了一个普遍现象，反映了教会间合作的教训和优势。一个城市中可能有三个华人教会，每个教会都使用不同的方言，而且来自不同的文化背景（通常是香港人、从台湾来的说普通话的人和台湾本省人）。由于成年人被语言和文化所分隔，因此他们的青年组也被分隔开来，尽管实际上他们会说一种共同的语言，即*西班牙语*。作为访问

53

dozen youth in each. Thereafter, we heard that the three groups apparently did not interact much, nor did they grow very much. This was a sad reality of ethnic problems among Chinese churches, complicating more important spiritual needs. But it reminds us to seek active cooperation with other churches to encourage and strengthen each other, especially important in helping to nurture the lives of the next generation.

3. Working with cross-cultural impact

I had heard that in a predominantly "white church" near us there was a very active youth minister who taught his youth strong Christian apologetics and academically tough classes, much more intense than the usual Christian youth group activities. I was intrigued, so I stopped by to join their Wednesday night services.

On one of my first nights I met Stephen, a young man in high school who was *giving* the evening's message. I was astonished that he was teaching as if he were a seminary professor, with very lucid points and lots of good handouts. I befriended Stephen and the youth minister, Ben, through lunch and coffee chats. Ben began to send over some of their more adventurous youth to visit with our church, and we began to invite him over to be a special speaker at our church.

So, both consciously and unconsciously, we developed a great informal mixture of Asian and non-Asian youth, especially the youth from Ben's group who had been well trained by him in apologetics and who later, amazingly, became great role models for our youth. Their names are practically legendary in our church lore: Avery, Greg, Stephen, Chad, Shawn, Jenny, all visitors initially, who then became integral members of our youth group, mission team members, youth counselors, and even youth ministers.

I joked to Ben that we had taken the "cream of the crop" of his youth group, in one way or another. He seemed pleased by the turn of events, pleased that his youth could serve the greater worldwide church. Over the

团，我们意识到他们主要是由于成年人的文化差异而被分开。这是一件可惜的事，对青年和青年事工也产生了副作用。至少，这就是我们这些局外人的感觉。

但是，只要我们辛城宣道团队到达现场，当地领导人就会大方地容许来自全部三个教会的年轻人参加我们的活动。这产生了出色的"群聚效应"，年轻人们轻松地使用英语和西班牙语交流，场面温暖人心。通常我们会进行一次联合的青年退修会，这对包括我们在内的所有人来说确实非常令人鼓舞和振奋。

但是可悲的是，当我们离开时，他们又分成了三个组。每个青年小组都太小了，可能只有十几人，无法有效地进行青年事工。后来我们听说这三个小组之间似乎没有互动，也不怎么成长。这是华人教会中因族群问题而出现的可悲现实，使如此重要的属灵需求变得复杂。但是它提醒我们，寻求与其他教会积极合作，以彼此鼓励和坚固，对帮助培养下一代的生活尤其重要。

3. 发挥跨文化影响

在我们附近的一个白人为主的教会中，我听说有一个非常活跃的青年牧师，向青年人传授基督信仰中的辨惑学和严谨的学术课程，比一般的青年团契更加讲究。我很感兴趣，于是在星期三晚上参加了他们的活动。

在最初去的某个晚上，我遇见了斯蒂芬。这名还在上高中的小伙子在那天晚上分享信息。让我感到惊讶的是，他好像一名神学院教授一样教导，观点很清晰，还预备了很多讲义。我通过午餐和喝咖啡的时间结识了斯蒂芬和青年事工牧师本。本牧师开始派遣他们

years, indeed we continued to "borrow" (is "steal" too strong a word?) much of their "top talent". I would assume that, *in hindsight*, if we were thinking of some kind of a win-win scenario, which I really *wasn't*, Ben's youth likely also learned many cross-cultural lessons by joining with us, much as we learned from them. In addition, since I loved to bring youth on missions trips, it became natural to include these "white kids" as integral parts of our mission teams. For the most part, they had never been out of the country before, especially to far-away Asia, so this was a wonderful additional life experience for them also.

一个蓬勃发展的青年事工需要许许多多的青年辅导员，这里只是小部分来自不同国家的辅导员，除了美国外，他们还有来自马来西亚、南韩、台湾、新加坡、柬埔寨、香港和巴西的。

Many, many, youth counselors are needed for a thriving youth program; just a sample of youth counselor All-Nations backgrounds, including Malaysia, South Korea, Taiwan, Singapore, Cambodia, Hong Kong and Brazil in addition to USA origins.

一些比较喜欢冒险的青年去我们的教会拜访，我们也开始邀请他作为特别讲员来我们教会讲道。

因此，我们在有意和无意间，发展了一个由亚裔和非亚裔年轻人组成的非正式团体。非亚裔年轻人主要是来自本牧师的那个团契，他们在辨惑学方面接受过良好的训练，后来成为了我们教会青年人的榜样。他们的名字在我们的教会中几乎成了传奇：艾利、葛列格、斯蒂芬、查得、肖恩、珍妮。他们最初都是来访者，后来却成为我们青年团契的组成部分、宣道团成员、青年辅导员甚至青年事工牧师。

我对本牧师开玩笑说，我们以某种方式夺走了他青年团契中的佼佼者。他对这件事的后续发展很高兴，因为他的青年团员可以服事更广的普世教会。多年来，我们继续"借用"（用"偷"这个词语气是不是有点太强烈？）很多他们的"顶尖人才"。我想，*事后看来*，也许这是一种双赢局面，虽然我最初并*没有*想到。本牧师团契的青年很可能通过与我们一起学习了许多跨文化的经验，就像我们从他们身上学到的那样。此外，由于我喜欢带年轻人去宣道旅行，所以我很自然也会把这些"白人孩子"看为我们宣道团队的组成部分。他们大多数人以前从未出过国，尤其是到遥远的亚洲，因此对他们来说，这也是很棒的额外的生活经历。

4. 万国青年的概念

这类联合宣道的努力增强了我们不断发展的"万国青年"的概念，意思是从各国来、到各国去的青年。这一切增强了我的一个信念：如果教会学会彼此合作，尤其是不同种族和文化的教会，通过

4. Youth for All Nations concept

The combined mission efforts added to the flavor of our growing concept of "youth for all nations" (YFAN), meaning youth *from* all nations, *to* all nations. All this reinforced my strong impression that the church will grow if churches learn to work with each other, especially churches of different ethnicities and cultures, to learn great lessons from each other through "cross-pollination".

Many of these "white kids" and even our American-born Asian kids experienced rather strong culture shock when we went to places like Thailand, where the people, culture, languages and food were all radically different, more so than going to neighboring Hispanic locations in the Americas. Suddenly halfway around the world, our cross-cultural team experienced eating fried insects, hearing and speaking exotic native languages, interacting with multi-ethnic tribal minority children, and riding on gigantic elephants.

I have no doubt that these mission trips changed the lives of many of these teenagers from different backgrounds, so that when they later moved on to long-term mission work themselves, or to solid professional lives supporting missionaries around the world, the impact of these youthful, truly cross-cultural mission trips was indelible.

Just a caveat, short-term mission trips work only if we are serious, and are not just bringing kids on missions for a fun time. The key, I felt, was the serious nurturing and training before going. Fully preparing them well, I liked to say, was 80% of the value of the mission, so that they could fully absorb the cross-cultural lessons when they reached the field. Indeed, the general nurture and training of youth in the youth group in a *cross-cultural* setting in Cincinnati, was basically also like that, a small flame that could create a wonderful fire and momentum, a key inspiration for all of life.

to continue, please read part 2 in Chapter 4....

"异花授粉"的方式，彼此学习重要的功课，那么教会将会不断成长。

许多"白人孩子"、甚至是在美国出生的亚裔孩子，去到泰国北部这样的地方时，都经历了相当强烈的文化冲击。那里的人、文化、语言和食物都截然不同，当中的区别比去邻近的拉美地区更大。突然间，跨越了半个地球，我们的跨文化团队经历了吃油炸昆虫，说许多稀奇古怪的外来语言，与多种族部落的少数民族儿童互动以及骑巨型大象的历险。

我毫不怀疑，这些宣道旅行改变了许多来自不同背景的青少年的生活，因此当他们后来开始长期从事宣道工作时，或者从事了专业工作、能支持世界各地的传道士时，年轻时的这些真正的跨文化宣道之旅对他们的影响是不可磨灭的。

有一点需要注意，只有我们认真对待，而不仅仅是让孩子们度过愉快的时光，短期宣道旅行才会起作用。我觉得关键是在于旅程之前的认真培育和训练。我常常喜欢说，为他们做好充分的准备构成了宣道80%的价值，这样他们在到达现场时就可以充分吸收跨文化的经验。确实，在辛辛那提的*跨文化*环境中，青年团契的总体培育和训练基本上也是如此，一小团火苗可以创造出美妙的火焰和动力，能启迪他们生活的各方面。

请继续阅读第二部（第 4 章）……

翻译：Frank Wu

4. Organizing a Strong Youth Program II: YFAN Counselors as Role Models and Leaders

I. YFAN (Youth For All Nations) counselors

Our youth ministry was particularly blessed by the good mix of both Asian and white students and counselors. The cross-cultural mix invigorated and challenged everyone in many ways to think and act creatively, as a great preparation for modern life, especially with all its complexities related to backgrounds and cultures. To top it off, into all this mix of serious youth training and fun, especially related to the interaction with our major "partner church", we even had a cross-cultural, inter-church marriage, which as of this writing has just birthed a new baby, icing on the YFAN cake! Their courtship had even been activated on a Thai YFAN mission trip!

出色的泰国短期宣道队，呈现出团员和辅导员、亚裔青年和非亚裔青年的良好组合。
Great team on short-term Thai mission, reflecting good mix of youth and counselors, Asians and non-Asians.

Tha
Tea
06

4. 组织强大的青年事工（二）：作为模范和领袖的万国青年辅导员

1. 万国青年辅导员

我们的青年事工特别受惠于亚裔和白人学生和辅导员的良好融合。跨文化的融合以不同方式激励和挑战每个人以创造性的方式思考和行动。面对因背景和文化而变得复杂的现代生活，这是一种很好的准备工夫。除此以外，在这一切严肃的青年训练和有趣味的活动的混合中，特别是在与我们主要的"伙伴教会"的互动中，我们甚至促成了一段跨文化、跨教会的婚姻，就在我写这篇文章的时候，他们刚刚生了一个宝宝，更为万国青年锦上添花。他们的恋情甚至是在万国青年的一次泰国短期宣道旅行中发生！

但是在我们的教会开始的时候，我们没有太多"非亚裔白人"辅导员。那时我们青年团的规模要小得多，每隔一两年，就会有一些年轻人义务担任青年事工主任，然后再去其他地方工作。这些人几乎都是来自泰国、加勒比海、印尼、马来西亚、新加坡和北美的亚裔人。多年来，他们为我们的教会和年轻人创造了一个"万国"带领者的有趣*序列*。最棒的是，他们都是令人印象深刻的榜样，我相信，他们激励了我们许多年轻人。

在追溯这些多元文化的青年事工主任之后的发展时，我很兴奋

But in the beginning of our church, we did not have this contribution by many "white, non-Asian" counselors. We had a much smaller youth group then, and each year or two, some different young adult would volunteer as youth director, before he or she moved on to other locations. These youth directors were nearly all Asians, from Thailand, the Caribbean, Indonesia, Malaysia, Singapore, and North America. They created an interesting *sequence* of leaders from "All Nations" for our church and youth over the years. The best part is that they were all impressive role models who, I'm sure, inspired many of our youth.

When I tracked down what had happened to these multicultured youth directors, I was excited to find out that, as far as I knew, *every one* of them had continued to serve the Lord, in many countries around the world, just an amazing testament to their commitment and the grace of the Lord in blessing them, and us. As I'm writing this, I can even imagine each one of them in my mind, so precious are they in God's eyes! Asian YFAN themselves.

Each one of our youth directors or counselors, as role models, was key to the development of our strong youth program. The "pastor definitely cannot do it alone" especially applies to youth ministry. It is practically essential that there are enough counselors to be *mentors* of the youth, commonly needing, I think, at least one effective counselor for every 10 youth.

I am gratified that each generation of youth seems to be better fortified for college and life, as I see them increasingly join college ministries, much more than in the past, serving in leadership positions, including Asian campus ministries! Several of them have even become involved in top leadership positions, affecting the work on the national level. And, as anticipated, some are in overseas missions, serving especially in Asia and China. Youth for All Nations indeed.

2. Shawn, the white kid

The story of Shawn, a "white kid", is a great reminder of God's grace.

4．组织强大的青年事工（二）：作为模范和领袖的万国青年辅导员
4. Organizing a Strong Youth Program II: YFAN Counselors as Role Models and Leaders

地发现（根据我所了解的情况），他们*每一个人*都继续在世界各地许多国家事奉主。这是一个了不起的见证，表明他们委身事奉，并有主的恩典赐福给他们，也使我们蒙福。在写这篇文章的时候，我甚至可以在脑海中想像他们每一个人的模样，他们在上帝的眼中是如此珍贵！他们都是亚洲的万国青年。

我们每一位青年事工主任或辅导员都树立了榜样，是我们强大的青年事工发展的关键。"牧师绝对不能单独做这件事"的概念，尤其要套用在青少年事工上。有足够的辅导员来当青少年的*导师*是最基本的要求。我认为通常 10 个青少年至少需要一个能发挥功效的辅导员。

马克在场上高速奔跑，凝聚了他多年来从教会、青年团体、大学获得的经验和知识，进一步在国际的工作上发挥。

Mark on the field running at high speed, condensing all his years of experience and learning from church, youth group, college, to further international work.

令我欣慰的是，我们每一代年轻人似乎都在大学和生活中得到了提升，因为我看到他们有越来越多的人进入大学参加大学生团体的事奉，并担任领导职务，当中包括亚裔人的校园团契！他们中有些人甚至进入了高层领导岗位，参与全国性工作的决策。而且，一如预期，一些人去了海外，特别是在亚洲和中国，参与宣道工作。确实是万国的青年。

2. 白人孩子肖恩

"白人孩子"肖恩的故事，是上帝恩典的一个见证。他第一次

On his first visit to our church, he was supposed to meet his buddy, Stephen (one of the first "white kids" who had started coming to our ethnic church). That particular day, Stephen was supposed to be taking care of a Sunday School class of younger teens. But, for some reason he did not show up on time. However, the topic for that session was Buddhism, and Shawn had just taken a class on the subject. So, in providential fashion, he stepped up to the plate, and taught the Sunday School lesson in place of Stephen. That was his introduction to our youth group!

I had been "forewarned" by Ben, the youth minister from our neighboring church, that Shawn was a good potential "recruit" for our church youth ministry. I had not met him before, and for some reason, I thought he meant Sean, another very fine product of Ben's youth group, and I was looking forward to seeing Sean. So, I was very surprised when Shawn walked into the Panera restaurant and introduced himself. But no problem, we hit it off fabulously, and soon Shawn *was* a youth counselor, and later our youth minister, a wonderful addition to our ministerial team.

3. Cross-cultural adjustments

Some of these interactions between "white" and "Chinese" leaders needed some adjusting on our part, or both parts. When we were planning to invite Ben, the dynamic youth minister, to speak at our church, I suddenly remembered that he sported tattoos and earrings, presumably partly to encourage better connection with his charges. I approached the elder-ministers group first about this, to "pre-empt" any misunderstandings.

Together, we checked out the Biblical bases for his body ornament culture, even including biblical references at the time of Moses. (Men wore earrings back then, did you know that?) I wanted to make sure we did not shock our more conservative church unnecessarily. I think we were able to adequately prepare the youths' parents of this cultural adjustment. Both sides seemed to take the transition well, preparing the way for many years of

来我们的教会是为了见他的好朋友斯蒂芬。斯蒂芬是第一批开始来我们族群教会的"白人孩子"。那天，斯蒂芬本应该在主日学校负责一个由十几岁的孩子组成的班级。但由于某种原因，他没有准时到场。然而，那堂课的主题是佛教，而肖恩刚刚上了一节关于这个主题的课。于是，就像出于上天的安排那样，他挺身而出，代替斯蒂芬讲课。那是他加入我们的青年团的方式！

来自我们的邻近教会的青年事工牧师本已经"预先警告"过我：对于我们教会的青年事工，肖恩是一个很有潜力的"新兵"。我没有跟肖恩见过面，还误以为他指的是他们青年团的另一个优秀成员辛恩（在英文里，Shawn 与 Sean 的发音是完全相同）。我一直很期待见到辛恩。所以，当肖恩走进潘娜拉餐厅并介绍自己时，我很惊讶。但是没有问题，我们相处得非常好，肖恩很快就*成为了*青年辅导员，后来又成为我们的青年事工牧师，大大加强了我们牧师团队的阵容。

3. 跨文化的调整

"白人"领导者和"华人"领导者之间的一些互动，需要我们这一方或者双方做出一些调整。当我们计画邀请充满活力的青年事工牧师本在我们的教会讲道时，我突然想起他身上有纹身，还戴着

阿祖和他的家人。在阿祖成长的时期，我们的青年团体模规仍然非常小且富有挑战性，现在他参与了全国性的校园事工。
Joe, who grew up in a time of a very small and challenging youth group, now serving in national campus ministry, with his family.

great cooperation and true fellowship! Meaningful inter-church cooperation, especially a cross-cultural one, needs healthy investments of time, patience and love. And maybe some forewarnings about cultural peculiarities.

4. Space issues

The good Lord even blessed us with lots of space, something very helpful to grow a strong youth program. I have always felt strongly about the need for lots of classrooms and some kind of gym in order to allow good interactions in the youth group. A gym was thus built soon after our first church construction, and was always put to good use by both young and old. After we had a major expansion of the youth group, we soon also found a Baptist church just across the street from our northern branch church. The church was very gracious to allow us to use their facilities on Friday night, when, in any case, they did not have any church activities. This was just perfect, since this church had an adequate chapel, lots of classrooms, 2 basketball courts, and even a fellowship area just right for Friday night snacks (including Chinese snack food!), something which the youth really appreciated. This worked out well for years, and was minimally expensive, again a great gift from God.

5. Bicultural elder

I have always felt that a bilingual and bicultural elder kind of person could significantly help the youth minister or counselors, especially if they are non-Asian, in relating to the predominantly ethnic Chinese parents and church leadership, particularly in the initial development of the youth program. In my case, I thought my role included playing "defense" and "interference" when necessary, a useful buffer in case of cross-cultural tension.

Indeed, over time, we received active parental help, mostly moral

耳环（大概是为了与教会附近社区的青少年建立更好的联系）。我首先与我们教会的长老牧师们交代了这一点，以"先发制人"的方式避免之后造成任何误解。

我们一起查阅了圣经中有关他的身体饰品文化的依据，甚至包括摩西时代的圣经内容。（那时的男人会戴耳环，你知道吗？）我想确保我们不会不必要地让我们倾向保守的教会感到震惊。我认为我们能够让年轻人的父母为这种文化调整做充分的准备。双方似乎都顺利接受这一转变，为多年的良好合作和真正的友谊铺平了道路！教会间要实质地合作，特别是跨文化的合作，就需要正面地投入时间、耐心和爱心，也许还包括一些关于文化独特性的预警。

4. 场地问题

上帝甚至赐予我们很多场地，这一点对发展一项强大的青年事工很有帮助。我一直都认为要有大量的教室和多功能的体育馆，青年群体才能进行良好的互动。因此，在我们第一次建造教堂后不久，就建了一个体育馆，使无论年轻人还是年长者都从中受益。在我们扩大了青年团的规模之后，我们很快发现在我们北部分支教堂的对面也有一座浸信会教堂。这个教会非常大方地允许我们在他们没有活动的星期五晚上使用他们的设施。这真是太完美了，因为这个教堂有一个足够大的礼堂、很多教室、两个篮球场，甚至还有一个专供周五晚上吃小吃（包括中式小吃！）的地方，这是年轻人非常喜欢的。多年来，这种方法一直奏效，而且成本最低，这也是上帝的一份大礼。

support, such as helping with transportation, providing snacks, and even as backup counselors as necessary. In general, we preferred that the *primary* youth counselors were younger where possible, since youth are in such a state of flux themselves and needed all kinds of role models. Godly Christians who were closer in age to them provided a significant perspective that they might not have at home. So, in general, the youth group program became a mix of predominantly Asian youth, predominantly "white" youth counselors, and Asian parents, all working together in a fascinating way!

6. YFAN impact

The whole effort was such a lot of fun for me, with many trials and challenges, but immensely meaningful. Especially when we saw the kids grow up and move away into "real life", into "All Nations", many with serious commitments to serve God. I always trust that the messages in their hearts will never be forgotten, since the word of God never returns void! Especially, I believe, when Godly messages are received in the critical formative years of youth.

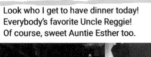

Look who I get to have dinner today! Everybody's favorite Uncle Reggie! Of course, sweet Auntie Esther too.

失散已久的前青年团员突然带著孩子和丈夫在西雅图出现，场面何等温馨。耶和华的话永不落空。
Long-lost contact, former youth, suddenly appeared in Seattle, with kids and husband in tow, how sweet indeed, Facebook 2018. The word does not return void.

5. 双文化长老

我一直觉得为非亚裔的青年事工牧者或辅导员搭配一位操双语和具双文化背景的长老，特别是在青年事工的初期发展上，能够大大地帮助前者与华人家长和教会领导层建立关系。就我而言，我认为我的角色包括在必要时扮演"防御"和"干涉"的双重角色，在有文化冲突的情况下，这会是有效的缓冲。

事实上，随着时间的推移，我们得到了很多青年父母的积极帮助，主要是精神上的支持，比如提供接送、零食，甚至在必要时充当后备辅导员。总的来说，我们更希望*核心的*青年辅导员尽可能地年轻一些，因为年轻人本身就处于这样一种不断变化的状态，需要各种各样的榜样。在年龄上与他们更接近的虔诚基督徒提供了一个重要的视角，这是他们在家里可能没有的。因此，总的来说，青年小组计画变成了一个神奇的混合体：以亚裔为主的青年团员、"白人"为主的青年辅导员和亚裔父母，所有人都一起工作！

6. 万国青年的影响

所有的努力对我来说都充满乐趣，虽然经历了许多考验和挑战，但意义非凡。特别是当我们看到孩子们长大了，投入"真正的生活"，进入"万国"，许多人都致力事奉上帝。我始终相信藏于他们心底的信息永远不会被忘记，因为耶和华的话永不落空！特别是，我相信，假如上帝的信息是在青少年这个成长的关键时期被接受的话，就更是如此。

翻译：DG

5. Youth Apologetics Ministry: Bunkers or Siege Engines?

Ben Walker

Pastor, Northern Hills Christian Church,

Cincinnati, Ohio

From the Editor: Ben Walker has been a wonderful colleague in ministry. His unique leadership of youth for over twenty years is an inspiration to many, and especially to me. I have firmly believed for decades that an essential component of raising a new generation is preparing youth for life through strong Christian apologetics training. Ben is the exemplar par excellence in this approach. One key reason our youth program has been going strong for decades is the help Ben has personally given to us in this regard. I am especially grateful that he allowed us to skim off the "cream" from his own youth program graduates. These young men and women, well trained in apologetics, have served our youth program faithfully and imaginatively, over many years, as counselors, teachers, and later even ministers. I am so glad Ben is able to contribute this essential article for this book, which also helps illustrate his great passion for youth ministry.

The Lord forged my faith in a university setting that was often quite hostile to God. It will come as no surprise to those believers who've been through the college experience, that the Adversary often strongholds in hubs of power and influence, and the university is nothing if not a center of power and influence. I was one of thousands of Christians who entered that setting and swiftly discovered this entrenched animosity. I learned the hard

5. 青年辨惑学事工：
是地堡还是攻城武器？

作者：本·沃克

俄亥俄州辛辛那提北丘基督教会牧师

编者注：本·沃克是一位出色的宣道同工。他以独特的方式带领青年，已经超过 20 年，这种方式启发了许多人，我就是其中之一。数十年来我都坚信扎实的基督教辨惑学训练是教养新生代青年不可或缺的基石。本牧师在这方面是首屈一指的模范。他亲身给我们的帮助是我们青年事工能经过数十年屹立不摇的重要原因之一。我特别感谢本牧师允许我们从他的青年培训结业生身上学习他的事工的精华。我们可以说是将他最优秀的学生"抢走"了。这些受过良好辨惑学训练的年轻男女都曾在我们的青年事工里担任教师或辅导员，甚至后来担任牧者，带着创意忠心地服事了多年。我很感谢本牧师为这本书写下这一篇重要的文章，这也显出他对青年事工怀着莫大的热诚。

主在一个多数人敌对上帝的大学风气里铸造了我的信仰。这对许多上过大学的信徒们并不陌生，敌人通常都稳坐于大学权力和影响力的中心，而不能成为权力和影响力中心的大学也算不得什么。我和数以万计基督徒进入了这个环境并立刻察觉到这种根深蒂

way that nearly any display of my faith invited attack, and found out, much to my chagrin, that the church hadn't prepared me to meet these attacks. Like so many Christians I thought I'd just cower my way from class to class, get my degree and get out. But the Lord had other plans.

"How come we never talk about this stuff in church?" a teen mused to a friend as I stood amidst a cluster of teens discussing all sorts of challenges to the Christian faith. This was more than a decade after I had finished college, but I was back on a college campus, this time at the front of a class as the instructor. I was attending an annual Christian conference for teenagers hosted by universities across the United States, having brought thirty or so teens from the church at which I was now a minister. The conference organizers, who knew of my rather specific ministry passions, offered me the opportunity to deal with difficult questions from teens, and had put together an elective class for just that purpose.

I taught for more than an hour to a room loaded with teens in every seat, on the floor, standing in the back of the conference room, and spilling out into the hallways. Now the session was over and this was their free time; they had the run of a college campus for several hours, but apparently it was more important to them to resolve their philosophical, historical, emotional, and scientific conflict with their beliefs. They must have been academic elites, right? No, just typical teenagers trying to make sense of life. There were atheists, agnostics, deists, and life-long Christians. The discussion with that group of fifteen or so lasted for almost two hours beyond our session. This was not unusual; I've had similar circumstances dozens of times in my ministry -- honestly, nearly every time I've had the opportunity to run a session like this.

The session I had taught was titled something like *"Ask Anything"* and was intended as an open question-and-answer forum where I would field questions from students about anything and everything related to Christianity. In these sessions we get questions like *"Why did God let my grandma die in front of me?"*, *"Who created God?"*, *"There are so many religions;*

固的敌意。我从惨痛的经历中学到我信仰的每个表现几乎都会招来攻击，我也很失望地发现我以前在教会里学到的并不足以对抗这些攻击。我像许多基督徒一样想要在课业里过一天算一天直到完成学业。但是上帝对我有不同的计划。

"*为什么我们在教会里从来没有讨论过这些事情？*"一位青少年若有所思地问他的朋友，当时我正站在一群青年人之中，他们都讨论着基督徒信仰面对的各种考验。那时我大学毕业已超过 10 年，我是以讲师的身分回到校园站在讲台上。我带着我当时牧养的教会里大约 30 位青少年参加一个由美国各地大学赞助、为青少年而设的基督徒年度会议。主办单位知道我专注的事工方向，于是给我机会回答青少年的棘手问题，并为此安排了一门选修课。

我在课堂里讲了一个多小时。当天座无虚席，学生们必须席地而坐，还有多人站在教室后面，甚至外面的长廊。讲习结束后就是他们的自由时间。他们有数小时的时间可以在校园里自由活动，不过他们觉得更加重要的是，要解决他们的信仰与哲学、历史、情感和科学之间的冲突。你觉得他们肯定是高材生吗？不，他们只是一般在寻找生命意义的青少年。他们有些是无神论者，有些是不可知论者，也有些从小就是基督徒。我和大约 15 个人在课后又讨论了将近两小时。这种情景屡见不鲜，自我事奉以来已经遇上这种情况几十次——坦白说，我几乎在每次这类讲习结束后都会遇上。

我的讲习主题有点像是"*有问必答*"。在那些讲习里我会回答学生们所有有关基督信仰的疑问，例如"*上帝为什么让我的祖母在我面前过世？*""*谁创造了上帝？*""*世界上有这么多宗教，我为什么要相信基督教是真的？*"或者"*上帝既然知道人要下地狱，祂为什么还要创造人？*"我多年的事奉经验告诉我，青少年有各种各

why should we believe that Christianity is true?" or "*Why would God create people knowing they would go to Hell?*" One thing my decades of ministry have taught me is that teenagers have questions. More often than you might imagine, those questions are exceedingly deep ... Sometimes these questions threaten their confidence in God. Here's another thing I know: the church has traditionally not done a very good job in encouraging students to ask those questions and then helping them to discover answers.

Shouldn't we just have faith? Well ... what is faith? Seems a simple question, but answering that question will radically alter how we function in the church. For many, "*faith*" means something like "*lack of doubt*" or even "*belief in spite of the facts*". This, however, is not what the Bible means when it describes faith. The Greek and Hebrew expressions could best be conveyed as "*a reasoned/reasonable trust*". It is not mindless belief, but rather a reasonable belief based on evidence and experience. How do you come to trust your parents? How did you come to trust your spouse? How does one find a reasoned trust in one's children? Is it not innumerable little engagements and small actions that engender a reasoned confidence? Daily experiences that compound to make you think this trust, this confidence, this faith is as reasonable as expecting that the sun will rise tomorrow. That kind of trust comes not just from a chosen belief, but also from doubts that are thwarted. This distinction [unreasonable belief vs. reasoned confidence] can make or break an individual's encounter with Christ and His church.

Let us return to my college years. At one of my first class sessions in the world religions department, the professor asked everyone to share why they were intending to study the particular religion that day. The first student volunteered that she had been part of a church growing up but that she hadn't felt there was much to it, and so was interested in trying something else. The second student said that he'd been raised Catholic and gone to a Catholic school, but wasn't impressed with Christianity and was searching to see what other religions had to offer. On and on it went like this, with nearly every student in the room expressing some tie to Christianity and then some

5 . 青年辨惑学事工：是地堡还是攻城武器？
5. Youth Apologetics Ministry: Bunkers or Siege Engines?

样的疑问。这些疑问的深度通常超过我们的想像。这些疑问有时会动摇他们对上帝的信心。我还知道另一件事，那就是教会一般并没有好好鼓励青少年问这些问题和帮助他们寻找这些问题的答案。

我们不是理所当然应该有信心吗？但是……什么是信心？这个问题看起来很简单，但答案可以在根本上改变我们如何在教会里运作。对很多人来说，"*信*

聚焦于对真理的追求，深入地与青少年互动
Engaging youth intensely and close-up in pursuit of truth

心"就像是"*不存疑问*"，甚或是"*看见与信仰不符的事实后仍然相信*"。可是，这些都不是圣经里所描述的信心。圣经里的希腊文或希伯来文的本意更接近"*一种经过思考或合理的信任*"。它不是盲目地相信，而是通过证据或亲身经历后理性地相信。你是怎样逐渐信任你的父母？你是怎样逐渐信任你的配偶？一个人是如何合理地信任自己的子女？这些理性的信任不都是从无数细小的事情和经历累积下来的吗？日常生活的点点滴滴日积月累成了我们所认识的信任，这份信心就像相信太阳明天还会升起一样合理。这种信心不只来自我们主观的相信，更来自那些被推翻了的各种疑问。盲目相信和有理性的信任之间的分别可以成就或摧毁一个人与基督和祂的教会的关系。

现在来回顾我在大学读书的日子。我在世界宗教系最先学习的一门课的教授，叫我们每个人都分享为什么我们希望研究某一个宗

sentiment that it all seemed rather shallow, and that they were in search of something different.

I knew I was to be the last person answering that question and was beginning to sweat, considering what I could possibly say that would not deny my faith in Christ, but also wouldn't make me the favorite target for my professor and this mass of people who clearly *knew* that Christianity was not the answer. As the moment approached, the fellow sitting to my immediate left confidently stated his name, then said without any hint of shame, "I'm a Christian, and I know why I'm a Christian. I'm here to prove to myself again that my faith is the right one". Needless to say, I found my courage and my voice, and affirmed my faith as well.

During the course of that semester I learned to defend my faith gently and with respect. In other words, I had discovered the ancient Christian art of apologetics. *Apologetics* derives from a Greek term for "giving an answer" (1 Peter 3:15). It is the endeavor to answer the challenges that the world levels against Christian belief, by using the best philosophy, science, archeology, statistics, history, and most any realm of academics you can think of. What began as a practical defense of my beliefs in a religion class, soon became defending the faith in nearly every classroom I sat in. So much has been written and done in this regard, that I was astonished that I knew so little about it. I had been raised in the church; why hadn't we studied these things? What a blessing to discover that I was not being called to abandon my mind in order follow my Master but, rather, being called to engage it! What joy to discover that my God can be worshipped with mind as well as heart.

The Lord in His great wisdom provides all the evidence we need to sustain and encourage genuine belief, but not so much as to compel it. Allow me to be careful here to say that I believe the evidence is profound and strong, but not so strong that a committed skeptic can be overwhelmed (forced to believe). With that said, there are many inside and outside of the church whose experience of God will feel incomplete or inadequate unless they are engaging God in the mind. Thus the church needs believers willing to learn,

教。第一个举手的学生说她从小在教会长大，但是她不觉得基督教值得更深入了解，所以她想尝试了解别的宗教。第二个学生说他虽然在天主教家庭长大并且去天主教学校读书，但他不觉得基督教有什么特别，反而想看看别的宗教能提供什么。其他学生的答案大同小异，几乎每个学生都和基督教有关联但又觉得基督教似乎颇为肤浅。所以他们都在寻找不同的宗教。

我知道我是最后一个回答的学生，所以开始冒冷汗。我在思考我应该怎么回答才不会否认我对基督的信心，同时也不会让我成为教授和同学的众矢之的，他们显然*知道*基督教并非答案。快轮到我的时候，我左边的同学充满自信地说出他的名字，并且毫不羞愧地说：“我是一个基督徒，我知道我为什么是一个基督徒。我来这里是为了再一次证明我的信仰是正确的。”当然，我也找回了我的勇气和我应该说的话，也重申了我的信仰。

在那一个学期里我学会了用平静和尊重人的方式保卫我的信仰。换言之，我发现了辨惑学这门古老的基督信仰艺术。*辨惑学*这个词的英文 apologetics 是源自希腊词，意思是“提供答案”（彼得前书三 15，和合本译为“回答”）。它的目的是使用最好的哲学、科学、考古学、统计学、历史，或者是任何一门我们可以想到的学问，来回答这个世界对基督信仰发出的各种挑战。最初我只是在宗教课里务实地保卫我的信仰，后来我几乎在所有上过的课里都得这么做。有关这方面的文献和研究多不胜数，我很惊讶自己对它们竟然几乎一无所知。我从小在教会里长大，但是我为什么从来没有学习过这些？我不是要放弃理性、反而是要运用理性才能跟随我的主——能发现这一点是何等大的福气！知道我可以同时用我的心和我的理性来敬拜我的上帝，是何等喜乐的事。

believers who will be a fountain of these philosophies and evidences, feeding the fellowship God places them in, and answering the skeptics that the Lord brings to them.

I ended up getting degrees in sociology, philosophy, and comparative religion with the intention of becoming a professor, but was stopped short when a church asked me to apply for a youth ministry position. After some wrestling with the Lord, I decided to go into vocational ministry in the churches with a determination to make apologetic training a central feature in my work with students, particularly in preparing them for the challenges they would inevitably face in the university setting. The eldership in the first church that ordained me seemed a bit skeptical about my vision for youth ministry, as conventional wisdom said that if you want to acquire and retain students, you must give the lion's share of attention to games and entertainment.

The church leaders gave me six months to attempt my ministry vision, and praise God, our youth group of 4 became 40. (These were serious students from both within and outside of the church, all with serious questions, broken lives, and challenges.) While the numbers were enough to sway our leadership, I want to be careful to offer a warning here: numbers are not the goal. Consider that Jesus was not impressed by numbers and arguably drove some away in favor of working with only serious disciples. (See John 6.)

I approach ministry with an agenda of forcing faith struggles with our students to occur in the context of the church, before they go off to universities and careers. To this end, we make students defend their faith, we diligently study other world religions and worldviews, comparing them to Christianity, and we study not just evidences to support the faith, but also the best arguments against Christian belief (so that students will have a ready answer when these questions hit in college).

Concerning games and entertainment, these things are fantastic when they hang on the skeleton of sound and challenging training in the faith. However, without that core, such entertainment is spiritually dangerous.

5．青年辨惑学事工：是地堡还是攻城武器？
5. Youth Apologetics Ministry: Bunkers or Siege Engines?

主用祂崇高的智慧给了我们足以支持和维持真正信心的确据。这些确据的数量足够却又没有多到我们必须强迫自己相信。我郑重地在这里说，我相信这些确据是深刻有力的，但是它们没有强至一面倒地压制一个坚定的怀疑论者（迫使他相信）。虽然如此，很多在教会里或者在教会外的人，若没有通过思考去接触上帝，就会觉得他们与上帝的交通并不完全或不充分。因此，教会需要愿意学习的信徒。他们要成为这些学问和确据的源头，滋润上帝给他们的肢体团契，并回答主带到他们中间的怀疑论者所提出的问题。

结果我拿到社会学、哲学和宗教比较学学位，原本计画成为大学教授，但是当时有一间教会邀请我应征他们一个青年事工牧师的职位。与主搏斗了一段时间后，我决定投入教会的全职事奉，致力将辨惑学训练作为我的学生工作的中心，特别是装备好他们面对将来在大学里不可避免的挑战。第一间按立我做牧师的教会的长老们对于我对青年事工的看法似乎有一点怀疑，因为传统的思维是：若想吸引和留住学生，就应该特别注重游戏和娱乐。

那间教会的长执会给我六个月时间来尝试我对事工的理念。感谢赞美上帝，我们的青少年小组从 4 个人增长到 40 个人（这些都是来自教会内外很认真学习的学生，他们有着严肃的疑问、破碎的生命，也面对着生命里不同的挑战）。虽然这个数目改变了长执会的印象，但我在这里慎重地给你们一个警告：人数不是我们的目标。要知道耶稣没有被人数影响，我们更可以说祂把一些人驱走以便专注于认真的使徒身上（请看约翰福音六章）。

我的事工的做法是让学生在尚未进入大学或者职场前，迫使他们在教会环境里与信心争斗。为达到这个目的，我们让学生捍卫他们的信仰，我们认真学习世界各国的宗教和世界观并拿它们来与基

Witnessing this more common *entertain-and-shelter* strategy, I've found that many of the students gained and retained through these means seem to disembark from their Christian voyage at the next most entertaining stop (usually in college or slightly before). I would describe these young folks as "cultural Christians": those who identify with a Christian group and can answer some of the important questions of faith in the "right" way. That is to say, they can parrot the right answer even when they can't explain what makes it right. In creating such folks many of us in the church feel like we've created a disciple, but these look nothing like the disciples in the New Testament.

Creating a cultural Christian is not unlike building a bunker. The idea is we put all the good stuff inside, and then build up fortifications outside that keep the students from being harmed or affected by the world out there. The goal is to keep these student's "*right opinions*" intact until they die or the Christ return -- you know, so they can say: "*look at what you gave me, I kept it hidden so no one would threaten what was yours, O God.*" (See Matthew 25:24-28; the Lord was clearly *displeased* with this answer and said as much.)

有些概念还是得靠深思所带来的皱纹才能扎根
Sometimes thoughts need frowns to imbed deeply

督信仰比较。我们不只学习支持我们信仰的确据，也学习各种反对基督信仰的有力论点（这样，学生们在大学里被问到这些问题前就已经有了答案）。

至于遊戏和娱乐，如果是建立在坚固而有挑战性的信心操练的骨干之上，也是很好的，但是如果不以此为核心，娱乐对我们的灵性是危险的。

我发现若是采取这个较常见的*娱乐与庇护*的策略，基于这个策略而来到并留下来的许多学生，似乎都只是为了下一个最有趣的港口（通常是大学或者大学之前）而离开他们的基督徒旅程。我形容这些年轻人为"文化基督徒"。他们自视为属于一个基督徒群组，也可以"正确地"回答一些有关信仰的重要问题。我的意思是说他们可以重复一些正确的答案，却没有办法解释为什么他们的答案是正确的。这一类人的出现可能令很多在教会里的人觉得我们教出了门徒，但是他们完全不像新约里的门徒。

教导出一个文化基督徒就好像在建立一个地堡。我们把好的东西放在里面，然后在外面建起坚固的防御层来保护我们的学生们不被外面的世界影响或伤害。目的是保存学生的"*正确看法*"，直到他们离世或基督再来，这样他们就可以说："*主啊，请看，我把你给我的藏了起来，这样就没有人能危害到你的东西了。*"（请看马太福音二十五 24-28；主显然不喜欢这个答案。）

反之，我们看到耶稣在新约里训练祂的门徒有正确的思路。祂所用的方法不只是告诉他们应该思考什么，还问他们能颠覆他们世界观的问题（读基督的话时，注意祂有多常向祂的门徒和那些挑战祂的人发问）。耶稣不只训练门徒如何保持他们的信心，也要求他们在信心上长进（请看马太福音十 16-17）。*祂惯于建造灵性的*

By contrast, in the New Testament we see Jesus training his disciples in right thinking, not just by telling them what to think, but also by asking them questions that would flip their worldview on its head. (Read the words of Christ with an eye on how often he asks questions, both of His disciples and of those who challenge Him.) Jesus didn't just train disciples in how to retain their faith, but demanded that they advance the faith. (See Matthew 10:16-17.) *He was in the habit of creating spiritual siege engines, or battering rams* to break into enemy fortresses. Now you might be thinking that analogy seems overly aggressive... after all, aren't we all sheep standing amidst wolves? Our New Testament fathers in the faith call us to a war of ideas, to wage war against every idea that sets itself up against the knowledge of God, and we're told that the gates of Hell will not prevail against these "sheep". We are called to be innocent as doves but to remember we are shrewd (careful/cunning) as serpents. Our Father delights in making the weak things mighty! (See Ephesians 6:10-17, 2 Corinthians 10:3-5 and Acts 17:22-ff, Acts 18:4,19.)

So, fellow believer, I leave you with this question. Are you trying to just keep kids in the church, or are you creating disciples who pose a threat to the adversary in his strongholds? Are you building bunkers or siege engines?

Note: Photo captions supplied by book editor.

攻城武器，以攻破敌人的堡垒。你可能觉得这个比方太过有攻击性……但是，我们不都是站在狼群里的羊吗？我们新约里的信心先祖呼召我们加入思想的争战，对一切攻击上帝的知识的思想宣战，我们也被告知地狱的门是不能战胜这些"羊"的。主吩咐我们要驯良像鸽子，但是记得我们也要灵巧（小心或精明）像蛇。我们的父喜欢把软弱的变为有力（参看以弗所书六 10-17；哥林多后书十 3-5；使徒行传十七 22 及下，十八章 4、19）！

因此，主里的同伴，我问你这个问题：你是试着把孩子们留在教会里，还是在装备门徒，使他们能威胁敌人的大本营？你正在建造的是地堡，还是攻城武器？

注：图片说明由本书编者提供。

翻译：Edison

6. White Pastor in Chinese Church: The Big White Bridge

Shawn Isaacs

Youth Pastor, Cincinnati Chinese Church

"Are you prepared to be wrong even when you're right?" said the wise, seasoned Pastor.

I was. And I wasn't.

"You'll never truly belong here," he added, himself a white American Pastor. I listened, but disagreed. If the Gospel is true, wouldn't barriers of race and ethnicity be broken down? Certainly, different races and cultures do belong together if the Gospel is true, I reckoned.

"Yes," I said. "Of course, no problem!" I said to his warnings. Excited to have the opportunity to start working as a Pastor, no obstacle seemed too great, no problem too significant. My interview (or interrogation, as it felt!) ended soon enough, and after months of meetings and prayer, I was the Youth Pastor of the Cincinnati Chinese Church. The white, American, 23-year-old, chubby Youth Pastor of a congregation that valued ethnicity, seniority, and physical fitness, among many other things. I'd fit right in!

I did. And I didn't.

After the honeymoon period, problems emerged. I did not fit in. My wife was not the Pastor's Wife Chinese churches expect -- she was not a free employee, nor was she going to lead all the children's activities. My kids were loud, liked hugs, and knew nothing of Chinese social mores. Other church kids were quiet and reserved. I'm emotional. Some believed emotions to be a

6. 华人教会里的白人牧师：白色大桥

作者：肖恩·以撒斯

辛城教会青年部牧师

"**即**使你是对的，但仍会被认为是错的，为此你准备好了吗？"——明智且经验丰富的牧师问我。

我准备好了，但也没准备好。

"你永远不会真正属于这里。"这位白人美国牧师说。我听见，但不同意。如果福音是真确的，不是应该打破民族和种族的障碍吗？我认为，如果福音是真确的，那么即便是不同的种族和文化，也该属于同一国度。

对于他的警告，我回答："我明白，没问题！"对于即将开始全职牧师的工作，我深感兴奋。在此时，没有障碍翻不过，没有问题克服不来。我的面试（感觉或像是审问！）很快就结束了，经过几个月的会面和祷告，我成为了辛城教会的青年部牧师。白人，美国裔，23岁，胖乎乎的青年部牧师，带领的会众重视族群性、辈分和身体素质等诸多方面。我可以胜任的！

是这样的，但也不是这样。

蜜月期过后，问题出现了。我并不适应。我的妻子不符合华人教会对师母的期待——她不是免费雇员，也不打算带领所有的儿童活动。我的孩子很吵闹，喜欢拥抱，对华人的社交习俗一无所知。

sign of weakness. My preaching led youth to know God more deeply and love Him more truly. But it did not always result in more measurable obedience at home, which parents sometimes desired even more than the salvation of their children. Another Pastor even accused me of "Americanizing" the youth. Maybe I had, but I supposed their growing up in America was responsible for that. I was by no means the Pastor they expected, but I was the Pastor who had committed to loving and serving their youth.

In spite of the problems, joys were innumerable. It took nearly a year for the church to decide to have me on as a Pastor but, once affirmed, I had their respect and support. I have been humbled deeply by youth and parents alike pouring out their hearts to me. Fears that their children would wander in college, fears that broken relationships would never be healed, fears that parents would never love them or think they're good enough.

A critical moment in working cross-culturally came on the Psychiatric floor of the Cincinnati Children's Hospital; it captures both the joys and the challenges of cross-cultural ministry. Chris (not his real name) had been admitted after making suicidal threats. He was not truly suicidal, but was exhausted and tired from all the pressures cast upon him. His parents were scared and did not understand what they had done wrong -- they'd worked so hard and provided him with so many opportunities, opportunities far beyond anything they'd ever had! After listening to him and to his mother it became clear to me -- *they love each other but keep failing to communicate love in meaningful ways.*

Mom worked to provide opportunities such as learning a musical instrument and going to college after high school graduation. Chris, meanwhile, simply wanted a hug and to be told, "I love you." Chris showed his love through words and physical embrace. Mom, meanwhile, wanted obedience, and she wanted to know that in the future her son could take care of himself. As we sat together in a bright, white hospital room, I was able to help each one see the acts of love the other had shown. Slowly but surely, the light in the room became nothing compared with the light in their eyes as

教会的其他孩子则安静而保守。我不掩饰情绪与情感，但有些人认为这是一种软弱的象征。我的讲道使青年人更加深刻地认识上帝，更真心地爱祂。但这并不能保证他们在家会更服从父母，而父母有时会重视孩子的服从过于孩子的救恩。另一位传道人甚至指责我将华裔青年"美国化"。也许我有，但我更认为主因是他们在美国长大。我绝不是他们所期望的牧师，但我是致力爱护和服务他们的青年孩子的牧师。

尽管存在问题，但仍有无数喜乐。教会花了将近一年的时间接纳我为牧师，一旦接纳了，我就得到他们的尊重和支持。这些父母与青年都同样对我倾诉心声，令我深感荣幸。有些父母担心孩子上大学后会迷失，担心破裂的关系永远得不到修复，有些孩子则担心父母不会再爱他们，或认为父母总觉得他们不够好。

学校毕业后，选择了一条非比寻常的路。
A graduation destination different from the usual path.

在这份跨文化的工作里，曾有一个关键时刻，那是发生在辛辛那提儿童医院的精神病学楼层。这个事件具备了跨文化事工的挑战与喜乐。克里斯（化名）因为企图自杀而要入院。他其实不是真的想自杀，而是因为所有加在他身上的压力令他困倦。他的父母吓坏了，不知道自己做错了什么。他们一直辛勤工作，为孩子提供了很多机会，这些机会远远超出了他们过去拥有的！在分别听完他和他母亲的说话后，我很清楚：*他们彼此相爱，但却没有用正确的方式表达爱。*

they truly began to see that they really did care for one another. Feeling loved, her love, Chris was inspired to obey his mother's wishes. Feeling loved, his love, his mom was inspired to tell her son she loved him.

No matter someone's ethnicity, age, or health, people long to be loved. To belong. To have their fears and tears wiped away. It doesn't matter if a church is African-American, Hispanic, or Chinese -- people yearn to be loved. Cross-cultural ministry is like lowering a raised draw bridge. Two sides are convinced each one is doing and saying the right things but no one can go anywhere, no progress can be made, because the two sides are fixed and locked in an upright position. They're not connected. It's the Pastor's role to slowly help lower the bridge so both sides can fulfill their purpose. Communication of love and truth can then pass from one side to another like cars and trucks going back and forth across the bridge to new destinations.

有些信息是需要翻译的
Some messages need translation.

I've asked many youth, "Do you feel more American or more Chinese?" In nearly all cases the response I get is, "It depends on where I am!" They're Chinese at home, American at school. But what about at church? This is where a major conflict emerges. On the one hand, parents are present. The kitchen smells like a Chinese kitchen. The walls feel like a Chinese home, lightly and efficiently decorated. But friends and peers are also present. English is spoken and heard.

As a white Pastor, I have to admit my limits in guiding the youth through this struggle. Navigating issues of identity is critical to cross-cultural ministry. Youth have told me they were concerned when the church brought in a white Pastor because I would not understand their struggles and would not be able

妈妈努力提供各种机会，像是让孩子学习乐器，让他在高中毕业后上大学。但是，克里斯想要的只是一个拥抱，以及妈妈口中的一句"我爱你"。克里斯通过言语和拥抱表达他的爱。可是，妈妈却想着要孩子听话，想确保儿子将来可以自己好好照顾自己。当我们坐在明亮的白色病房里时，我帮助他们看到对方表达爱的方式。渐渐地，病房里的光线都失色了，因为他们的眼里闪烁着光芒，他们在这一刻真切地看见彼此是非常在乎对方的。克里斯终于感受到爱，这样的爱让他愿意顺从母亲。他的母亲也感受到爱，因为儿子对她的爱，她终于说出她爱他。

不论种族、年龄或健康状况，人们都渴望被爱，渴望一份归属感，渴望有人能消除他们的恐惧、擦干他们的眼泪。不论教会的会众是非裔美国人、西班牙裔还是华裔，人人都渴望被爱。跨文化事工就像放下一座吊桥（译按：这里指的是一种开合桥，能从两岸收起桥身，使底下的大型船只通过，再放下接合）。两方都相信对方在做正确的事情，说正确的话，但却没有任何的沟通与交流，因为双方都是固定的、锁定在直立的位置。他们没有连接起来。牧师的角色是逐渐帮忙把桥梁降低，使双方都能达到自己的目标。这样，爱与真理的交流就可以从一侧传递到另一侧，正如桥面上来回往返的汽车和卡车一样。

我问过许多年轻人："你觉得自己是美国人还是中国人？"几乎所有情况下，我得到的回答都是："这取决于我身在哪里！"他们在家里是中国人，在学校是美国人。但是教会呢？这是让他们在身分认同上产生挣扎的地方。一方面，父母在场，厨房闻起来像华人的厨房，墙壁上简朴的装饰，感觉就像是华人的家。但是朋友和同伴也都在场，而且使用英语沟通。

to truly relate with them. There's truth to that! But I can also be a wise, trusted American in their lives who can help them work through that aspect of who they are.

"万绿丛中一点红 " 的白人牧师
A rose Pastor among many.

It doesn't matter that I take off my shoes when I enter my house, that I have high academic expectations for my kids, or that I love Chinese food. I'm not Chinese! But I don't have to be Chinese to pastor these youth. Being a white American has its obstacles in cross-cultural ministry, but it's also a great asset, as I can help parents better understand their kids' American tendencies, and I can likewise help the youth own that facet of their own identity. More importantly, I can direct everyone's attention to the Cross, the foundation of one's identity. Christ must come before culture, and all pastors, working cross-culturally or not, must be sure to model this in their own lives as well.

A temptation of cultural churches is to put serving the culture above serving Christ. At times the church seems to be a Chinatown of sorts, a place where congregants can escape American culture and retreat to the familiar and the comfortable. (To be fair, the same can be said of American churches -- retreating from the "sinful world" to a safer space to consume sports and entertainment.)

But there's immense joy and blessing in being a cultural church -- as a cultural church we recognize there will be some doctrinal differences, we know there will be some awkward gatherings, and we know there are some people present whom we must accommodate to include and to serve. As such, a commitment to being united in Christ is paramount for cultural churches.

Hospitality in the Chinese church is unmatched. "Love" may be

6．华人教会里的白人牧师：白色大桥
6. White Pastor in Chinese Church: The Big White Bridge

作为华人教会的白人牧师，我承认自己在指导青少年面对这种挣扎时能力有限。处理身分认同的问题，对于跨文化的事工至关重要。青年人告诉我，当教会邀请白人担任牧师时，他们感到担心，因为我可能不明白他们的挣扎，也无法真正了解他们。这是事实！但是我也可以成为一个明智、值得信赖的美国人，在他们的生活中帮助他们度过确认自我身分的历程。

我进屋时会脱鞋，期待自己的孩子在学校成绩优异，也喜爱中国菜，但这些都不重要，我仍旧不是中国人！不过，即使不是中国人，我也能牧养这些孩子。美国白人的身分对跨文化事工确实构成障碍，但这也是一项珍贵的资产，因为我可以帮助父母更加了解孩子的美国倾向，也可以帮助年轻人承认他们身分中的那一面。更重要的是，我可以将所有人引向十字架，那是构成每个人的身分的基础。基督仍是一切之首，理当先于文化，而所有牧师，无论是否涉足跨文化事工，都必须树立这种榜样。

文化教会（译按：一种有别于当地的主流文化的教会。此处指的是在美国的华语教会）面对的一种陷阱是服事文化过于服事基督。有时，教堂似乎是某种唐人街，在这里，会众可以回避美国文化，撤退到熟悉而舒适的地方。（公平地说，对美国教会也可以这样说——让人从"有罪的世界"撤退到更安全的运动和娱乐空间。）

但是，文化教会这身分也给我们带来极大的快乐和祝福——作为文化教会，我们认识到会有一些教导上的不同，我们知道会有一些尴尬的聚会，还有必须接纳和服事某些人。因此，对于文化教会，承诺要在基督里合一至关重要。

华人教会的热情好客无与伦比。要用说话来表达"爱"或会有点难度，但是毫无疑问，教会透过家庭聚餐、洗礼、庆祝农历新年，

challenging to verbally express, but there's no doubt the church shows it in the form of potlucks, baptism celebrations, and Chinese New Year celebrations. Cross-cultural ministry exposes one's own cultural sins but also reveals where other cultures magnify and glorify the name of Jesus.

Approaching ten years in the Chinese church, I still reflect back on the counsel of the wise and seasoned Pastor who prepared me for ministry. He was right -- there have been many occasions when I have been wrong even though I was right.

Having a network of other pastors and mentors has been essential to ministry. Being able to unload on others outside of the church has helped me be more loving, more spiritually and emotionally present for my congregation. Knowing I am covered in prayer and encouragement gets me through the darkest of days. Pastors without a support system won't last long.

But do I truly belong?

I do. And I don't.

One of the greatest compliments I received was when a mom greeted me with "Ni hao!" instead of "Hello!" She saw me as a part of the church, a part of the Chinese church family.

But I'm not Chinese. Thankfully, to belong, I don't have to be. I've grown in my love and appreciation for the church and the Chinese culture. They, too, have grown in their love and support of me in spite of differences. Problems will always exist, but this commitment of love and service to one another is true belonging, true partnership and fellowship, in the Christian sense of the word.

Note: Photo captions supplied by book editor.

也展现了爱。跨文化事工揭露了人们在自己的文化上的罪，但也透露了其他文化怎样赞美并荣耀耶稣的名。

在华人教会中待了将近 10 年，我仍然回想起那位为我做好事奉准备的牧师的忠告。这位明智而又经验丰富的牧师的那句话是对的——在很多情况下，即使我是对的，我还是错了。

与其他牧师和导师形成一个彼此支援的网路，对于事工至关重要。能够向自己教会以外的人卸下重担，使我对我

无可匹敌的待客之道
Difficult to beat the hospitality.

的会众更加充满爱心，在精神上和情感上都更加活跃。大家为我祷告和给我鼓励，所带来的支持与保护，帮助我度过了最黑暗的日子。毕竟背后没有支援系统的牧师，是无法长久持续下去的。

但是，我真的属于这里吗？

我是，但也不是。

我得到的其中一项最大的称赞，就是有个妈妈用中文向我打招呼："你好！"而不是用英文说"哈罗！"她把我视为教会的一部分，也是华人教会家庭的一部分。

但是，我仍然不是一个中国人。庆幸的是，我不必成为中国人，也能归属这里。我对教会和中国文化的热爱和欣赏与日俱增。尽管有分歧，他们对我的支持和爱也不断增长。问题将永远存在，但是从基督信仰的意义上来说，这种彼此相爱和服事的承诺是真正的归属感，真正的伙伴关系和团契。

注：图片说明由本书编者提供。

翻译：庄文菁

7. "You're So Naughty, One Day You Will Be a Minister"

Often I crack a joke to church kids when they are naughty: "You're so naughty, one day you might become a minister!" God uses all kinds of people, and sometimes it does seem like He takes the naughtiest kids, and makes them into ministers or missionaries.

Then there is the dramatic story of Saul, who became Paul, the Apostle. Saul was more than naughty: as a young man he persecuted the very early church. But when God's light shone on him, he instantly changed, and he became the premier evangelist of his time, writing most of the books of the New Testament, and suffering much in his lifetime for his Lord.

As part of the 40th anniversary of our church in Cincinnati, I illustrated this point by recounting the stories of three of "our kids", whose names are altered to "protect the innocent".

El was always getting into trouble. My son, Trev, was always the innocent little kid tagging along with the older El, who was often trying to teach him to do things he shouldn't do. One day, Trev was visiting with El, and El made this dramatic scene that his dad was very upset, and Trev should quickly hide under his bed. He described how his dad had this furious temper, and he was sure that he would be beaten severely. Then he ducked out of the room where Trev was crouching under the bed, and went into the next room, presumably to bravely meet his father's anger. Then Trev heard horrific screams from El being beaten by his father, who, incidentally, was a highly respected elder of the church. Finally, the yelling stopped, and El came into

7. "你这么顽皮，
终有一天会成为传道人"

我经常开玩笑地对教会里顽皮的孩子们说："你这么顽皮，终有一天可能会成为传道人！"上帝使用各样的人，有时候祂好像真的拣选了最调皮的孩子们，使他们成为传道人或宣道士。

后来成为使徒保罗的扫罗，他的故事就是那么戏剧性。扫罗不止是顽皮，他年轻时迫害了最初期的教会。但是当上帝的光照在他身上以后，他即刻改变了。他成为了当时最重要的福音传播者，写下了新约里的大多数书卷，并且甘心为了他的主毕生承受许多苦难。

在辛城教会 40 周年庆的时候，我回顾了教会里三个孩子的故事，来说明我的论点。为避免他们太尴尬，以下我用化名来称呼他们。

艾尔经常闯祸。我的儿子宪材常常只是无辜地跟随着比他年长的艾尔，而艾尔就经常教他做一些他不该做的事。有一天，宪材去找艾尔。艾

扫罗原本迫害基督徒，要他们接受审讯并被处死刑。但当耶稣在扫罗前往大马士革的路上向他显现，扫罗的生命有了戏剧化的转变。扫罗成为保罗——那位伟大的宣道士。图片取自谷歌安全搜索。Dramatic change in life: after a life of persecuting Christians, resulting in trials with severe sentences including death for them, Saul had a dramatic change in his life. When Jesus appeared to him on the road to Damascus, Saul became Paul, the great missionary. From Google Safe Search, all uses. https://farm2.staticflickr.com/1396/5076259214_9a6e4f16d5_b.jpg

the room sheepishly; quietly, he told Trev to leave by the back door, and not to tell anyone how vicious his father was.

Of course, we found out later that El had been beating the table with a belt himself, while he screamed out his cries of anguish.

El became a respected youth director, youth speaker, English congregation minister, and Chinese church senior pastor. Perhaps El's dramatic creative skills gave him great insight into how kids function, and obviously great story-telling abilities!

对于鞭打，爱恶作剧的孩子们有着源源不断的想像力。此图是华盛顿西雅图艺术家莉莉·海因曾的作品。
Mischievous kids have fertile imaginations about whipping. By Seattle artist Lily Heinzin.

Exhibit 2: Jos was one of the brightest kids in the youth group and was made valedictorian of Walnut Hills, the highest scholastically ranked school in Cincinnati. He even composed a Christian song that he was, surprisingly, allowed to sing at his valedictory speech. This was a creative (even mischievous) action since, as we all know, public schools in America are very sensitive about anything religious. As a child, Jos had a devious streak; he would often be the master planner, devising schemes which pushed other young kids into action while he stayed behind the scenes and out of trouble. At the time, most of the youth were boys, so one can imagine the amount of trouble the boys easily got into, especially with such a good organizer.

God used Jos' creative skills and his fertile mind to strategize and plan, and he now serves on a USA campus Christian ministry at the national level.

Exhibit 3: Mic lost his father when he was just a child. His father disappeared during a swim in California. His mother was not a believer at that time, but was comforted by ladies of the church, who brought her to church. His mother recounted often that Mic was a terribly naughty boy, quoting his father's comment that his total score for three

尔大吵了一顿，说他父亲很生气，所以宪材应该马上躲到他的床下。艾尔形容他的父亲脾气火爆，并且说他一定会被痛打。说完，艾尔迅速地离开了躲在他床下的宪材，走到隔壁房间，仿佛要英勇地去面对他那怒火中烧的父亲。之后，宪材听到艾尔被他父亲痛打时凄厉的喊叫声。顺便一提，艾尔的父亲在教会里是一位很受人尊敬的长老。最后，呼喊声平息了，艾尔也像一只小羊般回到他的房间。艾尔轻声地吩咐宪材从后门离开，并且千万不要对任何人说他父亲是如何凶恶。

当然，我们事后知道其实艾尔是自导自演，一边用皮带鞭打桌子一边发出痛苦的叫喊声。

之后，艾尔一步一脚印地成为一位可敬的青少年事工主任、青少年讲员、英语堂的传道人，到今日他已是一间华人教会的主任牧师。艾尔戏剧性的想像力或许正好使他能够理解青少年的行为，也给了他很强的说故事的能力！

第二例。约斯是我们青少年组里其中一个最聪明的孩子。他是辛辛那提学业排行第一的学校核桃山高中的第一毕业生致辞代表。他还自己写了一首称颂耶稣的歌曲，并出乎意料地获学校批准他在毕业典礼时唱那首歌。这是一种创新甚至是调皮的举动，因为众所周知，美国的公立学校对和信仰有关的事都特别敏感。约斯在小时候有着狡猾的小聪明。他常常策划，促使别的孩子们去做他计画中的事，而他自己却躲在幕后，远离麻烦。那时候，教会里大部分青年都是男孩。因此，你可以想像他们在一个聪明淘气的策划者带领下可以带来多少麻烦。

上帝使用了他的想像力和源源不尽的想法，去做策画和计画。现在他在美国校园基督徒团契中负责全国性的工作。

subjects *combined* did not reach the pass mark. At home he did mischievous things like put rice into the clothes washer. At a friend's home he would go into the closet and empty out the clothes. His mother was just terrified what he might do when he visited a friend's home; she was never quite sure what might happen.

One day at the annual Children's Vacation Bible School, the elder's wife introduced the Lord to Mic. He went home and announced to his mother, "Today, I have a new Father."

After Mic became a believer, everything started to change: Mic started to put his creative naughtiness to good use. He would often sneak into public toilets and leave Christian tracts; this paved the way to his becoming active in Campus Crusade, an active ministry to college students. As part of his ministry, he was sent to East Asia and Albania, and finally now he is in US church ministry.

I guess we could interpret naughtiness as expression of an active, creative, and inquisitive mind, that when idled, results in unconventional

你永远不知道小孩子在你背后可能做些什么。此图是华盛顿西雅图艺术家莉莉·海因曾的作品。
You never know what some kids might do behind your back. By Seattle artist Lily Heinzin.

actions, or pure disobedience. The beauty of spiritual rebirth is that it re-channels these energies into creative pursuits for God. Impulses which left unchecked can bring disaster, can be transformed for good. Young people, if you're reading this article, I trust that your "naughtiness" can turn into good, bringing blessings to others. You might even become a minister or missionary!

迈克是第三例。迈克小时候就失去了父亲。他的父亲在去加州参加会议后抽空游泳时失踪。他的母亲当时不是信徒。教会里的姐妹们去安慰她并邀请她来教会。迈克的母亲常常回忆说他是一个非常顽皮的孩子，并引述他的父亲说迈克三个科目的成绩*加起来*还不到及格的分数。他曾在家里捣蛋，把生米倒入洗衣机里，到朋友家时也曾把朋友的衣物从衣柜里全部拿出来。每当迈克去朋友家，他母亲总是战战兢兢，因为不知道迈克可能做出什么事来。

　　有一天，在一年一度的儿童假期圣经班里，一位长老的妻子介绍迈克认识主。他回家对她母亲宣布说："今天我有一位新的父亲。"

　　他信主以后，所有的事都开始改变。迈克开始善用他富想像力的顽皮想法。他曾经常"潜入"公共厕所，在哪里留下基督教小册子。这为他将来在学园传道会里向大学生传道铺了路。他曾为上帝的工作被差到东亚和阿尔巴尼亚，现在在美国教会里事奉。

　　我猜想我们可以把顽皮理解为一个活跃、具想像力和好奇的头脑的一种表现；若不好好运用，就会带来不合常规的举动或者是叛逆。灵命重生之美就在于它将这些能量重新导向，为上帝做富想像力的事工。冲动不羁的行为可能带来灾祸，正面的导向则能带来好处。青年人，你若正在读这篇文章，我相信你的"顽皮"可以变成有益的，为他人带来福分。你甚至有可能成为一位传道人或宣道士！

翻译：Edison

8. The Joy of Mentoring

Being a mentor is such a privilege and joy. I have been a mentor to many, in highly academic medicine and in ministry. In each relationship I have learned many lessons, and experienced the great satisfaction of seeing young people grow closer to what he/she was "intended to be!"

The question often is immediately asked, how do you *spot* the person that you think would be a good mentee? How do you spot that zeal, that spark in the eye that means that this person is destined for a greater purpose in life? What characteristic has this person demonstrated that helps you to decide? How do you figure out the good from the bad in each person, since no one is perfect? In essence, how do you really (or can you?) estimate or guess the potential of a person?

I dare say that there is no fixed formula, there are no real guidelines, and truly, the mentor's life experience likely helps. Over time, I think instinctively, you can begin to see how some people are just born with special potential, or that in spite of limitations you sense that there is a deeper drive that you recognize, but others may not necessarily notice or even want to notice. It's just not something you can add up or compute mathematically. And the interaction between mentor and mentee is very important; the chemistry really has to be *just right* also. Some interactions just do not click, and will not really be a good fit. Such is life, and not everyone is destined to work together. Especially if this process is meant to be over a long duration.

I do like the conceptual mystery of "seeing into their eyes", just the special spark, the gleam, the dedication in their eyes, the determination to

8. 做导师的喜乐

做导师是一项殊荣，也是一种喜悦。我在医学学术研究领域及教会事奉领域，做过很多人的导师。在每一段辅导关系中，我学到了很多，也因为看到年轻人越来越长成他"该有的样子"，而感到很欣慰。

常有人问：你怎么能*判断*哪个人适合你去辅导？你如何能看到这个人的热情，就是他眼中那种闪烁的光芒，让人一看就好像知道这个人生来就是要成就有意义的大事？这个人有些什么特点，让你决定去做他的导师？没有人是完美的，你怎么知道这个人的优点缺点？总而言之，你怎样（或能否）估计或者推测一个人的潜力呢？

除非你能够深深地看透他们的眼睛，否则你怎么知道谁的眼睛里有火花、有那种渴望和决心？身体力行，结交很多不同文化的朋友，建立同心支持的团队。

How would you know who has that spark in the eye, that gleam and drive, unless you peer deeply into his eyes? On the move, making lots of multicultural friends and building home team support.

succeed in spite of all odds. Not everyone has that same drive, and if we can spot it and nurture it, that drive can become something truly remarkable. There's something about the eyes being the venue of the soul, some basic truth about that! Simple things, like eagerness to learn, basic teachability, humility, sincerity and trustworthiness, are critical. These might be assessed through previous practical experiences when working together, which are usually much more solid than any flashy academic or secular achievement! And pride or arrogance, definitely "goes before a fall", so any prideful issues are definitely a warning sign that alerts you to potential disaster ahead, in spite of glowing records!

观察他们行动。行胜于言。吃当地人所吃，能够适应很艰苦的居住环境。
Watch them in action. Actions speak louder than words. Learning to eat like the locals and adapting to different difficult living conditions.

At a couple of points in my life, I would also try some kind of light-hearted "test" on a potential mentee, before agreeing to the relationship. For example, in chatting initially with a potential mentee, I might talk faster and faster, on an increasing variety of topics, or even take a fast walk together into heavy city traffic, chatting as we go, even up and down stairs, to see how well we could communicate without missing a beat. This "stress test" gave me some feel of how flexible and adaptable the mentee would be in stressful circumstances, and it worked well, but it became a bit exhausting for everyone!

8. 做导师的喜乐
8. The Joy of Mentoring

我敢说在这方面并没有一个固定的公式，也没什么正儿八经的原则方针。实际上，这跟人的阅历有关。慢慢地，你就本能地看到有些人天生就有那种特殊的潜能，或者有时候，你虽然看到一个人的局限性，但是你也能够感觉到他内心深处的驱动力，这不是每一个人都会注意到或想去注意的。这东西不是可以用数学运算出来的。师徒之间的交流很重要，他们之间的化学反应也要*恰到好处*。有时候跟有些人交往，就是不投缘，你也能马上就知道这可能不合适。人生就是这样，不是每一个人都适合和另外一个人一起合作，尤其像这种长期持续的师徒关系。

我确实喜欢那种一眼看上的"眼缘"，这似乎有点神秘，就好像你在对方的眼里看到一种特殊的亮点、光芒，还有那种要排除万难把事做成功的决心。并不是每个人都有这样的决心和冲劲，如果我们能一眼辨识并加以精心培育，这样的决心就能成就有意义的事。有说眼睛是心灵的窗户，这说法有一定的道理！一个人的一些基本素养，例如对学习的渴望、愿意受教、谦卑、可信赖，都很重要。我们能够凭借过往一起合作的实际经验，来考察这个人，这些经验往往比那些耀眼的学术成就更重要。骄傲，或者傲慢一定会令人跌倒，所以任何涉及骄傲的问题绝对是一个警告信号，提醒你潜在的大问题，哪怕对方的记录很耀眼！

此外，有几次我在同意做一个人的导师之前，先做了些轻松的"测试"。举个例说，有一个候选对象，一开始跟他聊天的时候，我可能会用很快的语速，然后会不断地转换话题，甚至会带他去车水马龙的地段散步，我会走得很快，边走边聊，甚至上下楼也继续聊。这主要是想看看我和这个人之间的沟通是否合拍。像这样的"压力测试"让我能够感受到在这种压力比较大的环境中，对方有多灵

Once we agreed on a mentorship relationship, a key practical part is scheduling of steady regular sessions together. I set this up with a goal for a potential *long-term* relationship. It could be monthly or even two monthly sessions, but some specific regularity helps make it work. And, because I give high priority to this interaction, I try to adjust my schedule to the mentee schedule since often theirs is more complex and difficult to manage, and I don't want to discourage them.

In my personal life I have taken the initiative to *seek out* my own personal mentors myself, and I think that's ideal. But not every mentee knows that they can do that, and some mentees are intimidated by that. So, it's good to encourage a potential mentee sometimes by making the initial suggestion to meet, but don't make it too easy. Having set it up, I insist that they make the call, or drive to a meeting place, to demonstrate their desire to be mentored. It's a two-way street that includes, importantly, love with understanding from the mentor, but there's no need to spoil them. Also there may be different phases of life too, so that when one phase is over, it could be that your mentorship could transition to a more detached relationship. Something like when your mentee gets married, or graduates from a specific program, that could be a decision point, because many other factors will start coming into play.

爱冒险的年轻人，很容易适应各种环境，能跟着专业人士边工作边学习。
Adventurous, adaptable and learning on the job by working with pros.

活、适应力有多强。这种评估方式其实是很有效果的，但就是会令双方都很累！

一旦我同意做某个人的导师，很关键的一点是要有定期会面的时间。我会安排这些会面，目标是要能够培养一段*长期*的关系。我们可能每个月见一到两次。不管相隔多久，定期的会面是很有帮助的。因为我重视两人的互动，我常常会调整自己的排程来满足对方的需要，因为对方的日程往往更复杂、更难安排。我也不希望他们因为排程的问题而不会面。

在我个人的生活中，我也曾主动去*寻求*人做我的导师。我认为这是理想的做法，但不是每一个想要被辅导的人都知道可以这样做，有些人会觉得有点胆怯，所以有时候我会主动提议第一次会面，以此来鼓励对方。但是我不会让会面做得太随便。安排会面后，我会要求他们主动打电话，或让他们开车到我们会面的地点，以此来表明他们愿意接受辅导。这关系往往是双向的，导师要有爱心，能够谅解，但是没必要去宠他们。人生有不同的阶段，当一个阶段结束，也许你的这段辅导关系需要过渡到一种较疏离的关系。例如接受辅导的人结婚了，或者从哪个课程毕业了，往往可以成为一个重新考量的时刻，因为这个时候可能有更多的因素需要考虑。

以前我会在吃午饭或喝咖啡的时间来做辅导，当然这个方式是要双方都同意的，尤其是让接受辅导的人觉得合适。但是现在我主要是通过视频或者电话聊天来辅导，因为我和接受辅导的人一般都在世界不同的地方。我认为遥距聊天其实跟面对面差不多，也一样有效，而事实上对我来说也节省时间，因为以前一个月一次一个小时的聊天，可能需要我总共三个小时的时间，包括开车吃饭等等。但现在一个小时的聊天就是要花一个小时，这其实是一种很有效的

I used to do my mentorship over lunches or coffee, to be decided mutually, but especially by the mentee. But now I am doing it mostly over video or phone chats, because the mentees and I are now all in different locations in the world. Long-distance chats, I think, are nearly as effective, and in fact, for me it reduces my time commitments to that one hour of chatting, say monthly, whereas in the past it might take nearly a three-hour time slot to just chat with one mentee, including driving time, eating time, etc., so it's really quite efficient nowadays. Of course, it's always much better and more fun to have chats over lunch or coffee, face to face, and we should treasure that interaction whenever possible! Face-to-face body language still outclasses video chat language. Which beats disembodied voices in the air!

It's good to remind myself also that I am *not* the mentees' parent, and I have to learn to back off at times, so that they have enough space. For me, it's convenient that often they think that I'm *just their "uncle"* (that's my name anyway) and therefore I probably don't have an excessive authority figure problem. Occasionally one of my mentees who is from a more passionate culture might come to respect me so much as to even hug me tightly and proclaim, "You're my father," and that's awe-inspiring to know that someone can respect you that much. However, that's over the top, and maybe "uncle" is perfect for me, and probably the best compromise.

Indeed, our chats range all the way from life itself, marriage, and family news, to serving God and others. Indeed, it often could be like a family chat. I tend to start by telling about what's going on in my own life, my own anxieties and prayers, my work, my meetings, my stories. Meaning that I open myself up first, which helps to break the ice, and even indicate areas where I need special prayer and concern. I am only human and not a super-person, and this is one way we can learn to encourage one another. There often are good testimonies and stories mixed in there, which could be meaningful and gently encouraging. And mutual sharing might bring back great memories, which might even trigger my writing them up later into a "real" Uncle Reggie story.

One thing I am usually careful about is that I don't make our chat into a

方式。当然如果能够一起吃饭，或者一起喝咖啡面对面聊，那是最好的，也更有趣。所以，有机会的时候就应该尽量面见！面对面的聊天带着肢体语言，总胜过视频上的聊天，更胜过只有音讯的对话！

我也会提醒自己，我*不是*对方的父母，所以有的时候我需要学习后退，让对方有足够的空间。我把自己看成*只是他们的叔叔*，刚好大家也都叫我"叔叔"。所以我并没有把自己当成权威。其中一个接受我辅导的人是来自一个热情外向的文化，虽然是男性，也会紧紧地拥抱我，然后声称"你就是我的爸爸"，以此来表达对我的尊敬。如果一个人真的能这么尊重你，必让你受宠若惊，但也有点过头，也许"叔叔"对我而言是最合适的，也是最折中的。

事实上我们聊天的内容会涉及各方面，从生活、婚姻、家庭，到服事主和服事人，往往就像家人聊天。我一般会先讲一讲我自己生活里正在发生的事，我的忧虑、我的祷告、我的工作、我的故事。我会先讲我自己，开放自己，这样就能够破冰。有时候我甚至会指出我需要对方为我祷告和关心的事情。我也仅仅是一个人而不是一个超人。这样也是我们学会互相鼓励的一种方式。当然其中也会参杂很好的见证和故事，很有意义，也能够鼓励人。这样一起分享，常常会带来一些美好的回忆。有时候甚至会激发我把它们写下来，成为"真正的"曾叔叔的故事。

有一件事，我一般比较小心，我不会把我们的对话变成打探消息，好像在查户口一样，这样往往会让人感觉不舒服，甚至会让人不信任。我一般就是随着对方，他把话题引到哪里就哪里。假如对方认为可以讲敏感的话题，那当然好；但是如果他们不愿意讲，我也不会去提。我最不想的就是失去这种辅导的关系，因为这种关系

probing session that makes it sound like an investigation, which could lead to discomfort and even possibly trust issues. I just let it go wherever my mentees would like it to go. If they are comfortable talking about sensitive issues then that's wonderful, but if they don't want to talk, I don't get into that. Above all, I don't want to lose the relationship, which is probably much more important than anything else. In some ways it's still like working with youth. Learn to back off and not push an agenda, and let the discussion go naturally.

I really view mentoring best as "just coffee chats", indeed just like the title of my books. So there's no high expectation necessarily that comes with it, but if the time comes when there's a need, I am right there. Especially when personal issues, illnesses, and pains come up, I am there, hopefully like a member of the family, as someone who has been on this road before, and they can call on me as necessary.

Indeed, in times of crisis, I'm there to listen, to cry when crying is needed, to pray together, to give some advice for the marriage or ministry or work when asked. The "safe uncle" at a safe distance, not too far away wherever I am in the world. For as long as they like it; that's not a problem, it could indeed be for life. For instance, one of my own mentors has been a mentor practically for life, and it continues to be a great pleasure to see him or chat with him, even as now it's not as often as in the past.

For me, when I see *my mentees* grow up and living a very meaningful life, a life of contribution, that satisfaction and inner joy are just unmeasurable. We are very privileged to be able to be an earthly mentor, working together with the heavenly one. We can indeed be the theory and principles that have put on flesh and blood. Remember Jesus, the unique flesh-and-blood Incarnation, the greatest model Mentor, who mentored all kinds of people, even those whom others would not have instinctively felt were the "best material". But these somewhat unlikely people were changed themselves, and changed the world, from a handful, to a third of the world's population.

是最重要的。在某些方面，这就好像跟年轻人相处一样，你要学会什么时候该退一步，而不要步步进逼，顺其自然地聊天就好了。

我真的把这种辅导看成是"喝喝咖啡聊聊天"，就好像我出版的书名一样。所以我不会带着特别大的期待，必须聊什么，但当有需要的时候，可以随时问我。尤其是当他们个人遇上问题、生病、痛苦时，我会像一个家人一样陪伴。因为我自己也经历过这些，他们可以在需要的时候随时找我。

实际上当出现危机的时候，我会在那里倾听，我会陪他们哭，也会一起祷告。如果他们询问我，我也会在婚姻、事工或工作方面向他们提出建议。我是那位"安全的叔叔"，保持一个安全的距离，无论我在何处，他们都不会觉得太远，可以和我安全地聊聊。只要是他们喜欢，那就没问题，有时候更发展成为一种终身的关系。举例说，我自己有一个导师真的成了我终身的导师，我每次看到他或者和他聊天，都会非常开心，虽然我们现在也不像以前那样频繁地见面聊天了。

对我而言，当我看到*我辅导的人*成长了，过着很有意义的生活，成为一个有贡献的人，我内心就感到无法言表的满足和喜乐。我们很荣幸能够配合天上的导师，成为一个地上的导师。实际上，我们应该在地上实践天上导师的教导。谨记道成肉身的耶稣是最伟大的模范导师，祂辅导了各种各样的人，甚至是那些别人看来并非"理想人选"的人。但就是那些好像不可能的人却得着改变，也改变了世界。从一开始的十几个，演变成全世界三分之一的人口。

翻译：Dixia

9. Missions Emphasis in the Church: Start Young

"**D**avid Livingstone was poised with his rifle, kneeling down to watch out for the marauding lion, when suddenly, out of nowhere, the lion jumped into the air and landed directly on him. The lion roared, and opened his gaping mouth wide over the head of David Livingstone, and......... I'm soooo sorry, but tiiiime's up!" A huge sigh of disappointment rippled through the Vacation Bible School kids, as they shouted, "no, no, no." But *Vacation Bible School* has to go on, and there's always a tomorrow.

"猛狮正要吞噬大卫·利文斯顿的头颅（戏剧化的版本）。……对不起，下课的时间到了，明天继续说故事吧……也许要待明年的暑期圣经班……" 图片取自谷歌安全搜索。

"Lion about to eat Dr. David Livingstone's head" (dramatized version) .... I'm sooo sorry, time's up, we will continue the story tomorrow......... Or next year... at VBS...."

From Google safe search, all uses. https://www.flickr.com/photos/glenbowman/22943915863/

Often, on the last day of VBS, I might say at a critical point in the missionary story, "I'm soooo sorry, but we have to continue the story *next year*. Come back, next year! for Vacation Bible School!" After a resounding clamor of disappointment, I finally relent and *reluctantly* finish the story for this year.

Wouldn't you want to come to Vacation Bible School to hear missionary stories? Wouldn't you be touched by the story of David Livingstone, spending the best part of his life in darkest Africa? Or Adoniram Judson, kneeling on the deck of

9. 教会宣道的重心——从小开始

"**大**卫·利文斯顿一动不动，眼睛眨也不眨地盯住正在猎食的狮子……突然间，那头狮子跳起，扑到大卫身上。狮子大吼，向着大卫的头张开庞然大口……真的对不起，下课的时间到了！"唉……此起彼落的唉叹声在班上的孩子口中发出。这一群每年 7 月中来教会参加暑期儿童圣经班的小朋友不约而同地大声反抗说："不行！不行！" *暑期圣经班* 仍会继续，总是后会有期。

每年暑期圣经班的最后一天，我都会讲到一个宣道故事的高潮。"真对不起，时间到了。要听故事的结局，你们 *明年* 回来继续上暑期圣经班吧！"讲到紧要关头，我会突然停住。在一轮抗议声之下，我就故意 *勉为其难* 地讲完了今年准备的宣道士故事。

如果是你，你会来教会参加暑期圣经班，听宣道士到世界各地传道的故事吗？大卫·利文斯顿用了一生最宝贵、最年轻有为的几十年时间，到当时世上最落后的非洲去传道，你会被这个故事感动吗？再想想贾德森，他和年轻的妻子在去缅甸传道的途中，跪在甲板上，不得不为他们第一胎的早产婴孩举行水葬，把尸体投在海里。

辛城教会以往 25 年来每年都举办暑期圣经班，其中有五年我们录下了当时所讲的 *宣道故事*。在 YouTube 里输入 "Uncle Reggie Vacation Bible School Stories "，你就可以找到这些视频。你可以

111

the boat, as he and his very young wife on their missionary journey to Burma allowed their firstborn premature baby to be dropped into her watery grave.

Google "Uncle Reggie Vacation Bible School Stories" on YouTube, and you can watch a sample of these *missionary stories* given at Vacation Bible School every year for 25 years at the Cincinnati Chinese Church, and you will have a feel for why it is important to educate children when they are young, so that they begin to know that there is a wide world out there, a world of great needs and great potential, a world awaiting literally thousands of young people to bring the message of hope and love, so often lacking in many distant lands. There are real needs, *not imaginary story-book needs*, and what better time than *childhood* to let the next generation know. *Proverbs 22:6: "Train up a child in the way he should go, and when he is old he will not depart from it."*

Don't believe this *nonsense* about natives having their own beautiful culture, and having no need for outsiders to come in and mess up their culture. That's a whole bunch of propaganda spread by people who are living in a bubble, who are selfishly sitting in their armchairs living the American dream, philosophizing about "wonderful idyllic native cultures, unsoiled by Western values". They do not know what they are talking about, and mostly they have never lived for any significant period among the millions in this world who face many fatal childhood infections and diseases and who have little hope and little love. All the more reason to teach young children the truth about reality when they are young, so that they can dream big dreams!

We need to tell the great stories again and again. *Hebrews 12:1: "Therefore, since we are surrounded by such a great cloud of witnesses, let us throw off everything that hinders and the sin that so easily entangles. And let us run with perseverance the race marked out for us."* Try to *find a good story teller.* Encourage him or her to develop this talent as a ministry. Start with young story tellers when they are youths, when they are curious and enthusiastic. Give them lots of good books to read. Choose a story that is long enough, and detailed enough. Give the young person lots of flexibility to develop the stories. Give him or her permission to embellish the story, to add creative

看到为什么从小就教导儿童是那么重要，因为这让他们知道外面的世界很大，在世界中有太多的需要，正等待千万年轻人带着希望和爱的信息，去到那些偏远、未曾听闻这些信息的地方。这些都是切实的需要，和*童话故事书里讲的实在大有区别*。这一点最好让下一代在他们*年轻的时*候就能知道。*箴言二十二章6节："教养孩童，使他走当行的道，就是到老他也不偏离。"*

不要相信那些*荒谬的言论*，说土著自有美丽的文化，别让外来人进来搅乱他们。这是一些生活在保护罩内的人鼓吹的概念，他们自私地住在豪华的房子，有舒适的沙发，生活在安定无忧的现代化的美国梦里，幻想出"原始民族那些不受西方价值观污染、诗情画意的美好文化"。其实他们根本不知道自己在讲什么。他们自己没有花上一段相当的时间身历其境，在那样的环境里去体验那民族的生活，面对多种致命的小儿传染疾病，缺乏希望缺乏爱。正是这样，我们更需要趁小孩子年轻时教导他们现实的真相，以致他们可以在年轻的时候就怀抱伟大的梦想！

所以我们要一再讲述这些伟大的故事。*希伯来书十二章1节："我们既有这许多的见证人，如同彩云围着我们，就当放下各样的重担，脱去容易缠累我们的罪，存心忍耐，奔那摆在我们前头的路程。"找一位会讲故事的*。鼓励他或她发挥这项才能，建立一门事工。从年轻的说故事者开始，因为他们充满好奇，又热心。送他们很多好书让他们阅读。先选一篇长度适中、也细致入微的故事，让年轻人自由发挥，编成故事，穿插不同有趣的细节，加入这些民族的一些风俗习惯，不同的文化背景，当地美丽的风景和气候的特色，编成一个非常*有趣生动*的故事。只要能保持情节的真实性，不偏离原文，可以像所有好听的故事一样，加添艺术感，把骷髅头、土著

components of the culture, the language and the beauty of the land, in order to make the story even more *exciting*. Of course, be factually correct, but allow artistic license, as in any good story. Skulls, spears, snakes, and tarantulas are all part of the story.

Often I would throw rubber snakes and spiders into the screaming audience; they loved it. My favorite stuffed toy, a monkey named Abu, put in cameo performances every year and was a favorite of the kids -- except for one time when they were so enthusiastic they tore apart his right leg, so that he had to be stitched up in my wife's private clinic and rehabilitated. I can still see the scars on his poor little leg.

I usually think that 15 minutes at most, every day, is plenty to keep the attention of 100 boisterous children. I like to split the day up into three scenes of about five minutes each, in order to allow development of the story in each of the five-minute segments. It's great to have at least one major highlight per day and one good take-away message. Allow opportunities in the story to describe the struggles and challenges, dependence on God, and the joy of the gospel. It's all right if the missionaries all die from spears from the natives, because the children will know that there is a deeper message, and a long-term higher purpose. Sacrifice and patience for the long haul are important messages for any age. The Christian message can be costly, not just for Paul. *2 Corinthians 11:25: "Three times I was beaten with rods, once I was pelted with stones, three times I was shipwrecked, I spent a night and a day in the open sea..."*

The youth group kids are riveted when real live *missionaries visit* and spend special time with the youth. The youth were spellbound by the story of K&J, who were arrested by authorities in western Asia for helping the local church grow in homes. The prison guard told the husband that his wife had died in prison (which wasn't true) as a way to mentally torture him. One day, the prison guard softened up and claimed that he had had a dream of Jesus, and that one day he might even be a Christian, but then he would lose his job. And, amazingly, the presiding judge allowed the wife to tell the story of why she was so eager to let people know about Jesus, at the risk of her own

的矛枪、蛇、全身是毛的黑蜘蛛参入故事中。

我经常会带些橡皮制的蛇和蜘蛛，当提到这些小动物时，就抛进听故事的小朋友中，引起他们大声惊叫，更增加故事的生动情趣，小朋友也非常喜爱这些意外的插曲。我有一个布制的小猴子，是我讲故事的小助手，我给他取名叫"阿布"，每年都让阿布客串演出，孩子都爱它。一次，小朋友们争相拉扯阿布，结果阿布的一条腿给拉断了。我回到家，特别把阿布送到曾太太的私人诊所动手术，将他的后腿从新接上。自从那次意外事件后，阿布即使康复了，伤痕却仍然随着它。

我认为如果能保持将近 100 名精力充沛的小朋友的注意力，每天 15 分钟就足够了。我常常将讲故事的时间分成三段，每段五分钟，每段有不同的布局。最理想的是每天安排一个故事的高潮和一个让小朋友带回家去反刍思想的信息。故事里可以描述主角心中的挣扎和生活上的挑战，他如何依靠上帝，从上帝的话中得到喜乐。即使最后宣道士全都为主殉道，死在土著的矛枪下，也不伤大局。因为小朋友会知道有更深一层的真理，有更崇高的目标要达成。舍己和坚忍到最后，是任何年纪的人都要学习的一门重要的功课。传讲主的信息有时得付上重价，这不只是对保罗而言。*哥林多后书十一章 25 节："被棍打了三次；被石头打了一次、遇着船坏三次，一昼一夜在深海里……"*

当有*宣道士来教会作见证*，这些年轻人就完全被他们吸引住，我们也特别安排一些时间让年轻人能直接听他们的分享。当 K 和 J 夫妻二人提到他们在亚洲西部因为协助教会增长而被当地官僚拘禁的经历时，年轻人听得入迷。狱警告诉 K，他的妻子已经死在监狱里。但这其实不是事实，只是在精神上施加压力。一天，狱警软化

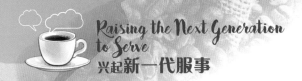
life, in a courtroom with many in attendance, who were then able to hear her heartfelt testimony. Afterwards she was set free. As they like to say, life is stranger than fiction. As the early disciples were witnesses, so today we can say amen to verses like *Acts 5:32: "We are witnesses of these things, and so is the Holy Spirit, whom God has given to those who obey him."*

Indeed, when the many international workers serving in difficult circumstances come to visit our church, we make a special effort to allow them time to *speak face to face* with the youth. The youth quickly come to realize that missionary workers are real live people who have real live problems, and that they are not some weird super-spiritual people. We who are living in a free society can be oblivious to what really happens in lands far away; these close-up encounters with missionaries give the youth much better perspective. And they see how the love of God can change people even in extreme circumstance, even hopeless situations. And the youth can see how difficult and challenging it can be to want to really serve the King of Kings. So, should they consider a life of service themselves, the youth can face potential challenges with open eyes, knowing that ultimately we have a Lord who promises to be with us, wherever we are, even in the worst of circumstances. They will learn the true meaning of the verses *Proverbs 3:5-6: "Trust in the LORD with all your heart and lean not on your own understanding; in all your ways submit to him, and he will make your paths straight."*

鼓励年青人参与短宣，像泰国短宣。这些参加过短宣的年青人，有不少后来都投入了事奉，成为"万国青年"。

Encourage youth to go on short-term missions, such as to Thailand: among short-term missions teams, significant numbers later go into ministry and service, as Youth for All Nations.

A young lady who decided to go into the mission field wrote a letter to our church mission committee, saying in jest that, "I blame Uncle Reggie...." While I never feel that I should be "blamed", I definitely do feel that it is my responsibility and that of the church, to make the mission world an obvious *opportunity* for

了，声称他作了个梦，梦中见到耶稣，并说可能终有一天会成为基督徒，但这样他就会为此失去工作。一天，奇怪的事发生了，法官竟然准许 J 在法庭上讲述她为什么那样热心地传讲耶稣，即使她知道这样做会对生命构成威胁。但也因此，法庭上有许多人都听到她从内心说出的见证。后来她获得释放。俗话说：人生有时比小说更奇妙。早期的使徒成为见证人，同样，今天我们也能对*使徒行传五章 32 节*这类经文说"阿们"：*"我们为这事作见证；上帝赐给顺从之人的圣灵也为这事作见证。"*

实在的说，很多在国外传道的同工都在一个很艰难的环境下事奉，当他们来到我们教会访问，我们尽可能安排机会让他们与我们的青少年*面对面地交谈*。青少年很快就察觉到宣道工作都是真实的人、面对真实的生活问题，而不是什么奇怪的超级属灵人。我们在国内生活在一个自由安全的环境里，可以完全忘掉在遥远的国度里真实的生活情况。与宣道士的这种面对面的交谈，能让这些年青人获得更恰当的观点，知道即使环境有多困难、情况有多绝望，上帝的爱都可以改变人心。年青人更可以知道，想事奉万王之王是多么困难和具挑战的一回事。因此，有一天如果他们也决定要终生事奉，就可以放胆面对可能出现的挑战，因为知道我们的主应许我们，不论在任何情况下、即使是最坏的环境下，祂都会与我们同在。他们会学到*箴言三章 5 至 6 节*的真正含意：*"你要专心仰赖耶和华，不可倚靠自己的聪明，在你一切所行的事上都要认定他，他必指引你的路。"*

一位决定要加入宣道工作的年青女孩写了一封信给教会的宣道事工小组，戏谑说："这都怪曾叔叔……"。我不觉得我应该被"怪罪"，但我确实觉得，那是我也是我们教会的责任，要将宣道事工

service, and potentially *one of the highest callings* that a person could have. Especially in an Asian context, the young people are already inundated with role models of doctors, engineers, finance advisors and IT specialists, sometimes to the deliberate *exclusion* of missionary service. However, I never direct a young person specifically towards the mission field. That calling has to be *God's call*, and not from others.

If young people feel called by God, I will of course help them discern the calling, and help prepare them for the obstacles and possible repercussions that might come their way. Everyone needs encouragement, and those entering a lifetime of missions will usually need special encouragement, since the road ahead is not easy. Often, parents will be the first to try to stop them, or objections will come from even close friends, or well-meaning people who declare that they do not have the "right qualifications". So, it can be an uphill battle, right from the start. Nevertheless, it is exciting to record that in 46 years of our church's existence, more than 60 people have been called into ministry or mission (excluding short termers), young and old, with *more than half of these before the age of thirty. 1 Thessalonians 5:11: "Therefore encourage one another and build each other up, just as in fact you are doing."*

I believe our churches definitely need to better provide a proper perspective of what the *entire spectrum* of opportunities are for young people to serve in their life journey. If our main goal in life for every Christian is to glorify God (Westminster Creed), then the mission field is clearly one of the most meaningful opportunities to glorify our Lord. Start buying lots of *missionary story books and give them as gifts* to the most faithful young people. And start a *missions library*, so that anything related to missions can be displayed there as a reminder of the importance of missions, from a really young age.

Those young people who do not go to the foreign mission field will be inspired to notice the many problems of society even in our own country, even right in our own backyard. And often they will later become the important long-term supporters of foreign and local missionaries, who might have

变成一个很好的服事*机会*，更是*其中一个最神圣崇高的呼召*。尤其是对于亚裔年青人，他们早已有一大堆医生、工程师、理财顾问和电脑工程师来作榜样，有时更刻意把宣道事工*屏除*在年青人未来可以选择的计划之外。但是，我从来没有明确地指引年轻人从事宣道工作，因为这是*上帝的呼召*，是从上帝来而不是从人来的。

如果年轻人认为上帝在呼召他，我会从旁帮助他们明白那是否上帝的呼召，并且帮他们做好准备，应对他们也许会遇到的阻力和负面的意见。每个人都需要鼓励，这些年青人如果选择奉献一生做宣道工作，更需要特别的支援和鼓励，因为他们前面的路是崎岖难行的。第一个尝试阻止的往往是父母，要好的朋友也可能会阻拦，或是一些持有善意的相识也会好言相劝，提出"你也许还不够资格"。一开始就有来自不同方向的阻力，如同行上坡路。尽管如此，令人兴奋的是，我们的教会在过去 46 年中有超过 60 位信徒被主感动加入了事奉或宣道的行列（不包括短宣），*其中超过一半在蒙召时是 30 岁以下。帖撒罗尼迦前书五章 11 节："所以，你们该彼此劝慰，互相建立，正如你们素常所行的。"*

我认为教会绝对需要提供一个恰当的角度，让年青人知道在他们的人生旅程中，能够参与事工的*各种*机会。假如每个基督徒一生的主要目的都是荣耀上帝（根据西敏斯特信条），那么宣道工场显然就是其中一个最好的机会，让我们荣耀我们的主。第一步可以是*购买宣道士的故事书送给最忠信的年轻人为礼物*。并且开设一个*宣道图书馆*，把一切与宣道有关的书籍杂志陈列出来，从小就提醒年青人宣道有多重要。

那些没有到海外宣道的年青人也能借着这些书刊的启发，留意到社会上的许多问题，在我们本国、甚至我们的邻舍中间发生。他

even come from their own youth group. Thus, an immediate and very tight connection is created between the field workers and their critical home-team support. Young people do grow up, you remember.

Mission committees are charged with the important work of promoting missions in the entire church. But, partly because the mission committee is often so busy connecting with and supporting existing missionaries, it can be easy to neglect children and youth, even though the mission committee should be the real driving force for future missions. Thus, the *mission committee* needs to be deliberately reminded to especially try to focus on *coordinating with the children's ministry and youth ministry* to develop mission consciousness in the children and youth. And when missionaries visit, we must make sure they include visits with the children and youth. Remember the Lord's rebuke of the disciples, *Matthew 19:14: "Jesus said, 'Let the little children come to me, and do not hinder them, for the kingdom of heaven belongs to such as these.'"*

In conclusion, we all know that youth is a time for idealism, and most great missionaries in the past have made their decisions to go to the mission field when relatively young, and physically left for the field in their late teens or early twenties. It is sobering that if you go to cemeteries of missionaries on the field, you will see the tombs of many young people, names you might not recognize easily since they died so young. Try visiting the Morrison Cemetery in Macau, the former Portuguese colony, now reclaimed as part of China. As you read the tombstones and note the very young ages of those buried there, including many children of missionaries, it is a reminder of the great sacrifices of young people that have brought Christianity to China. The sacrifice and cost today are different, and probably not so dramatic, but the challenges are similar. Be part of a movement to *raise up a new generation* to serve Him among the nations. Youth for all Nations.

们后来往往会成为重要的长期支持者，支援海外的宣道士，甚至是跟他们来自同一个青年小组的本土宣道士。就是这样，工场上的工人和本土教会的支持团队之间，就形成了一种即时且十分紧密的联系。要记住，年青人始终会长大。

教会宣道事工小组的责任之一是提倡全教会的宣道工作。可是，即使宣道事工小组应当是未来事工的真正推动力，它却很容易忽略了儿童和青年，部分原因是它往往忙于联络和支援现有的宣道士。所以，*宣道事工小组应该特别注意要协调儿童事工和青年事工，启发儿童和青少年对宣道事工的认识*。有宣道士来访问的时候，更须将儿童和青少年包括在安排的活动之中。谨记耶稣在*马太福音十九章14节*中谴责门徒：*"让小孩子到我这里来，不要禁止他们；因为在天国的，正是这样的人。"*

总结来说，我们都知道年青人是理想主义者，历史上最伟大的宣道士都是在年青的时候决定献身于宣道工作，而且不到20岁出头就启程投入宣道工场。拜访宣道士的墓地是件发人深省的事。你会看见许多年青人的墓碑，那些名字都是很陌生的，因为他们在非常年轻的时候就离世了。有机会可以去澳门拜访马礼逊的墓园。澳门过去是葡萄牙在中国的属地，现已回归祖国，你可以读读碑上的墓志铭，留意埋葬在那里的年轻人，他们有些是宣道士的儿女，提醒我们年轻人为将基督信仰带到中国而作出的牺牲。现今宣道士的牺牲和代价已经不同，也许不一定像过去那样献上生命，但在宣道事上的挑战和困难几乎和以往没有两样。让我们参与这场运动，*兴起新的一代*在各国中事奉祂，成为"万国青年"。

翻译：Tom King、Amy Zhao

10. Starting a Missions Effort

I have been inspired by missionaries since childhood. During the Second World War, when I was a baby, our family had to escape from Hong Kong, the city of my birth, into China. The Imperial Japanese had invaded the then-British colony, so Dad took us back to our ancestral Hakka village, in the mountainous areas of Guangdong Province. His father, my grandfather, had been the Gospel Mission Hospital Director in that village, and my dad then assumed that position during the War.

Because of my dad's job, our family lived on the mission compound, and missionary doctors and nurses became our family friends and neighbors. Later on, growing up in Hong Kong, our family also had many missionary friends who would come by to visit. So, it is little surprise that from early childhood I grew to know and appreciate the key roles of missions in the church and world.

In my mind, there is no question that missions is a fundamental component of church health, as emphasized by Christ's Great Commission. With the perspective of nearly five decades of church ministry, and after observing growing churches, I even like to say "no mission, no church". Or, "if we don't have missions, the church dies". It is that important. But, sometimes we think missions simply means sending financial support overseas. That is actually the simplest step. It is mission *involvement* that is so vital to our own spiritual growth. When we become involved in the lives of missionaries, we begin to truly feel real joy, especially as we see the wonderful blessings that come with missions. However, there is also the possibility of real pain. We

10. 开展宣道事工

我从小就深受宣道士启发。在第二次世界大战时，家人带着襁褓中的我从我的出生地香港逃到了中国。日本帝国占领了当时的英属香港。于是，父亲带我们逃到我们的祖籍地——广东山区的一条客家村。我祖父曾是村里那所教会医院的院长；二次大战时期，我父亲就接下了那个职位。

因此，我们全家都住在医院宿舍里，宣道士医生和护士就成为我们一家的朋友和邻居。后来，回到香港后的成长期间，也时常有许多宣道士朋友来我们家探访。如此，我从小就耳濡目染，逐渐认识并重视宣道在教会和世界所担当的重要角色，这一点也不令人意外。

在我心目中，宣道无疑就是健全教会不可缺少的组成部分，这是基督的大使命所强调的。以我 50 多年来在教会里服事的经验以及对教会成长过程的观察，我甚至会说"不宣道就没有教会"。换句话说，"我们若不宣道，教会就会死去。"宣道就是如此重要。不过，我们有时候会认为宣道不过是指以金钱支援海外事工。事实上，这只是最简单的一步。我们若要灵命成长，就必须参与宣道。当我们参与宣道士的生活，就能够亲身感受真正的喜乐，尤其是亲眼见到宣道所带来的奇妙祝福时，感受更深。然而，我们还有可能承受痛苦。可能我们不希望*在痛苦中学习爱*，但是我们有时候必须

may not like it when the lesson of *"love is painful"* happens, but it is usually only then that we can truly learn the lesson of love, God's love for the nations.

The minute we begin church missions, there are instantly *competing* tugs at our heart for many other church needs, near at hand, possibly staring us in the face; for example, the never-ending requests for church maintenance, renovations and building expansion. And if we are a very responsible church, local ministries also cost a lot. Often, the far-away missionary stands little real chance of financial and spiritual support in comparison with local needs. Missions truly needs unconventional thinking, and requires the full support of ministers, elders and deacons, especially from the most senior leadership; otherwise, it would be a weak effort.

But, missions can be great fun, so let us start with that. My decades of working in church missions included three decades specifically in China and Thailand, and close involvement with both new and established mission agencies. It has been a great experience, full of joys and pain. Right off, the biggest problem is its complexity; I would need several articles to cover it adequately.

From our church's very beginning, we began efforts in missions. We found it practical to focus on certain geographic areas, so as to not get too spread out or distracted, since mission needs are always very large in scope (like the whole world!). Asia was a natural focus for an Asian church, given our closer understanding of the cultures, as well as our natural connections. Another key area soon appeared to us, the Middle East and related areas, which was extremely challenging, but therefore likely *greatest in need*; we would learn many new lessons from missions to this area of the world.

We became interested in missions to the Middle East because of a Caucasian couple studying at the local University of Cincinnati; they came to our bible study because of their interest in northwest China minorities. They went on to serve in the Middle East, and are still serving there, after decades of ministry. And then we had a lady youth director who went on from our youth ministry to a similar region. Her courage was inspiring to us, since she

经历过才能学到爱的真谛，明白上帝对万国万民的爱。

在教会展开宣道事工的那一刻，我们马上察觉到教会里还有很多*别的事*需要我们劳心出力。这些事可能是教会的例行维修、翻新，又或者是扩建。再者，一个有负担的教会很可能已经在本地事工上投入了许多金钱以及精力。跟本地的需要相比，身在远处的宣道士能得到的财务或精神上支持的机会少之又少。因此，宣道事工需要跳出常理的思维，也要得到教会的牧者、长老和执事，特别是最资深的领导群的全力支持，否则就难以发展下去。

与宣道历史连接：著名的资深宣道士贝蒂·麦克基。1930/40 年间，她在贵州事奉，那是当时饱受战火摧残的中国其中一个最贫困的省份。结束在中国的服事后，她一如往常精神饱满地鼓励我们当时正在辛辛那提建立一个华语教会的工作。她将近 90 岁高龄时安息主怀。

A connection in mission history: very senior legendary missionary, Betty McGehee, who ministered in war-torn China, in one of the poorest provinces, Guizhou, in the 1930/40s, vivacious as ever until she passed away at nearly 90 years of age. She became a significant encouragement for our fledgling Chinese church in Cincinnati.

宣道事工可以是很有趣的。我们先从这里说起。在我数十年的教会宣道工作里，有 30 年是专注于中国和泰国事工，跟初创和既有的宣教机构都有密切的合作。那些宝贵的经历里充满着喜乐以及艰辛。事工的复杂性是一个大问题。这得要分成几篇独立的文章才能充分说明。

自我们教会创立时，就开展了宣道事工。我们发现因为事工需要可涵盖的地域十分广大（可以是全世界！），所以切实的做法是专注于特定的地域，这才不会把精力分散了。由于对文化的了解以及既有的关联，亚洲是亚裔人教会很自然的选择。我们很快也想到

was diagnosed with diabetes just a few months before she was due to go, and yet she was determined to go, and still serves there today.

And, there are other areas in various parts of the world with *high personal risk*, and therefore also among the most needful areas. For example, we had a couple planning to work in the highly risky border region of Northeast China and North Korea. Unfortunately, we lost contact with them after many years, likely because of the sensitive nature of their work. This was the only situation where we "lost" a worker. Another example would be a single brave lady working in the "slums" of Cincinnati, seemingly just as risky a venture, given the drugs, gangs and prostitution problems, a ministry we have maintained for decades, to this day.

We realized early on that if we were a solid Bible-believing church, practically by definition *some young people* should soon be eager for missions, and therefore should be given high priority. The first missionaries the church supported were indeed an American-raised, Cantonese-origin physician and his Taiwan-born wife, both of whom studied at our local university, destined for medical mission in Igbo, Nigeria soon after graduation.

Many of our young people destined for missions needed quite a bit of hand-holding, counseling and prayer support. Especially since nearly all parents in our first decades *instinctively balked* at the prospect of their *own* children "responding to the call". Since I was eager for missions, there was even a rumor going around church, warning serious youth, "don't talk too much with Uncle Reggie, he might get you into missions". In actuality, on the contrary, I have been dead serious that the missionary call should be a "God call," and definitely *not* a calling from an elder, no matter who he is.

Each young person truly had to struggle and wait patiently until their parents accepted their call, or at least did not directly obstruct them. Thankfully, all who were called were able to proceed, albeit many after a few years of struggles. Over the years, the growing numbers provided inspiring encouragement for subsequent youth to be even more open to full-time service.

了中东地区。我们知道在中东宣道是十分艰难的，但是正因如此，中东地区的*需要也是最大的*；我们也可以从中学到很多功课。

我们对中东宣道的兴趣是源自一对在辛辛那提大学读书的白人夫妇，他们最初是因为有心到中国西北部服事少数民族而来我们教会参加查经会。不过，他们后来决定到中东服事，至今已数十年。之后，一位在我们教会当青年事工主任的年青女信徒也决定投身那个地区服事。虽然她在去中东前几个月被诊断出患有糖尿病，但她仍坚决启程，在那里服事直到今日。我们很敬佩她的勇气。

世界各地还有其他地方*非常危险*，但因此也有着迫切的需求。例如我们有一对夫妇去了极危险的中国东北和北韩边界工作。可惜，多年后我们和他们失去了联络，这可能是因为他们的事工十分敏感。这是我们唯一一次"失去"了我们的同工。另一个例子是一位勇敢的单身女性，她到辛辛那提的贫民区工作，基于那里的毒品、帮派和卖淫问题，那同样是一项冒险的事工，但却持续了几十年，直到今天。

我们很早就认定我们若真的是一间坚定地以圣经为本的教会，教会里的*一些青年人*就应当对宣道事工有负担。因此，我们很看重培养青年人宣道。我们教会支持的第一对宣道士就是在美国长大、来自广东的医生以及他在台湾出生的妻子。他们两人都在我们本地的大学读书，毕业后不久即前往尼日利亚的伊博参与医疗事工。

我们最后决定投身宣道事工的年轻人，有许多都需要很多建议、辅导和代祷。这特别是因为在最初的十数年，几乎所有的父母都*本能地拒绝*接受*自己的*孩子"回应呼召"。因为我热诚于宣道事工，教会里甚至有传言，警告认真的年轻人"不要常和曾叔叔说话，他会把你带去宣道。"事实上，我对宣道的看法和传言刚好相反。

Somewhat later, another group needing missions support was early retirees. Their financial needs were much lower, or none at all, but they still should have the prayer support and encouragement of the church. My wife and I were privileged to respond to full-time missions at age 54, a great age for our "first early retirement".

YOUNG AND older full time for ALL NATIONS 为万国全职事奉的老中青			
MINISTRY 区域	YOUNG 青年	MID 中期	EARLY RETIREES 提早退休
USA 美国	14	9	5
CHINA 中国	6	2	8
AISA 亚洲	6	1	3
MIDDLE EAST 中东	3		
AFRICA 非洲	2		

万国青年事工：教会差遣到工场的人中，主要是以青年为主。

Youth for all Nations: predominance of youth versus older ages among the missionaries sent out to the field from our church.

Overall, the greatest joy was that in the first 46 years of our church history, over 55 individuals related to our church went on to full-time ministry, with over half of these being young people. And each new missionary automatically became a role model and example to others.

Many young missionaries-to-be had no experience with fund-raising, so they needed coaching on approaches to churches, committees, small groups, and individuals for support. "Non-Asians" often prefer more direct approaches (some agencies even teaching new recruits how to "close the deal"), but "Asians" prefer more nuanced approaches, so there were cross-cultural differences straight away.

I especially liked to encourage aspiring missionaries to have lunch or coffee with potential donors; this allowed a thorough one-on-one explanation of the missionary's calling and ministry needs. This personalized connection, even with a small group, left more lasting impressions and connections, leading to a precious and strong bond, sometimes for life. Of course, many missionaries-to-be needed help in overcoming their initial embarrassment and hesitation, but they did learn, literally on the job.

Church leadership and mission committee members definitely helped

我确信宣道的呼召必定要是"上帝的呼召",而绝对*不是*来自任何一位长老。

每一位青年人都必须经过挣扎和耐心等待,直到他们父母接受他们的决定,或者至少不直接反对或阻止他们。感谢上帝,虽然有些青年人要经过几年的挣扎,但所有被呼召的青年人最终都能如愿以偿。这些年来,逐年增加的数目让我们倍感激励,也鼓励了后来的青年人对全职事奉抱持更开放的态度。

再后来,另一组在宣道方面需要支援的人就是提前退休的人。他们对于财务支援的需求很低,有时根本没有需要,但他们仍然需要教会的祷告支持和鼓励。我和妻子就有幸能在 54 岁"第一次提前退休"时回应全职事奉的呼召。

总而言之,让我们倍感激励的是,在我们教会第一个 46 年里有超过 55 人投入全职事奉,其中过半是青年人,而每一个新的宣道士都自动成为后继者的榜样。

有志成为宣道士的年轻人多半没有筹募经费的经验。因此他们需要接受训练,了解如何向其他教会、委员会、小组,以及个人寻求支助。"非亚裔人士"一般喜欢比较直接的方式,有些机构甚至教导新人如何"完成交易";但是"亚裔人"比较接受间接的方式。这是文化上的差异。

我鼓励有志成为宣教士的年轻人主动和可能提供支持的人吃午饭或者喝咖啡,借此一对一地亲自向他们解说成为宣道士的呼召以及事工的需要。直接与个人或团体接触更可以留下持久的印象和关系,甚至能结出珍贵且坚固的情谊,持续一生。当然,许多年轻人都需要帮助,克服最初的尴尬感和踌躇,但我发现他们的确能边做边学。

make the connections for aspiring missionaries, to help them meet with individuals or small groups. The usual 7-minute (or 3- minute) presentation at Sunday service was helpful but "ceremonial", usually signifying a *blessing* by the church, opening the door for missionaries-to-be to meet freely with church members. The Sunday presentation usually raised little real support; in the long run, personalized interactions provided greatest support.

We learned from hard reality that there should be a support team of at least three in the church, willing to pray for each missionary seriously and regularly (even using the internet for prayer meetings) to provide spiritual support for the long haul. Otherwise, the missionary could later lose connection with the church, especially if there were mission problems, or changing membership in the mission committee or even in the sending church. We considered it so essential that, later in our mission committee, we insisted on a core team as *prerequisite* for approval of each missionary for support. In times of trials or special needs on the field, this core team became an *advocacy group* for the missionary, like a cheering team, helping to raise awareness, the "la la team" in Chinese.

10. 开展宣道事工
10. Starting a Missions Effort

任何职业都可以为上帝的爱作见证。音乐事工也可以有效地接触那些喜欢见到子女学习音乐的家庭。

All professions can be a testimony of the love of Jesus. Even music ministry can be effective in reaching families who love to see their children perform.

　　教会里的领导团队以及宣道小组可以帮助有志成为宣道士的人去接触别人或者是团体。主日崇拜后那些七分钟或三分钟的简报也有帮助，但只是在"形式上"表示教会的*祝福*，让准宣道士有机会和教会里的会众见面。主日崇拜的简报通常都未能招来实质的支持；长远看来，最大的支持是来自与他们有个人接触的支持者。

　　碰过壁后，我们学到教会里应该有一个至少三人的小组，愿意经常认真地（即使是透过互联网）为每位宣道士祷告，并且长期提供属灵的支持。不然，宣道士很容易与教会失去联系，特别是在遇到事工上的问题，或者是在宣道事工小组甚或教会出现人事变迁的时候，失联的情况更容易发生。我们很重视这一点，因此，后来我们的宣道事工小组坚持在批准支持宣道士之前，*必须*先组成一个核心团队。当前线宣道士遇到考验或者有特别需要时，这个核心团队就成为他们的*支持团队*，像啦啦队一样帮他们打气，使教会知道他们的需要。

翻译：Edison

11. Salt and Light

Jesus gave a colorful and apt instruction to his disciples, and to all of us by extension, that we are to be "salt and light" of the world. This expression has touched the hearts of many, and has deep meaning and implication for all of life. Personally, I have always loved this instruction, and it has essentially driven most of my life, wherever I go in the world. Salt, meaning to give flavor and interest to life, and to others; light, meaning to explain and help brighten the lives of those around us. The beauty of salt and light in action is also that we are blessed even more, as we bless others.

When we started our medical mission in China, MSI, 25 years ago, I thought that it was perfect that we could indeed have the potential to be salt and light, in a land that previously had been *closed* to the outside world. It was a relatively sensitive time, and salt and light seemed the perfect approach to help people in need, especially among minority tribes and in deprived areas. By our actions and our love, we were able to be helpful, and to learn many things by working with poor tribal people in the mountains of Southwest China.

盐、光、英语对话，和云南村庄的孩子们。
Salt, light, English conversations, and kids in Yunnan village.

11. 盐和光

耶稣给祂的门徒，包括我们所有人，一个生动而贴切的教导，要我们去做世上的"盐和光"。这个比喻打动了许多人的心灵，也有着深刻的意义和生命中的实用价值。我个人一直很喜欢这个教导；不管我在世上任何地方，在我的大半生中它一直激励我。盐，代表着给生活和他人添加滋味和乐趣；光，代表着解释和帮助照亮我们身边人的生活。若能发挥功效，"盐和光"的美也在于我们祝福他人的时候，我们所获得的福气更多。

当我们 25 年前开始在中国进行国际医疗服务时，我认为那是我们在一个对外*封闭*的土地上做盐和光的最佳机会。那是个相对敏感的时代，做盐和光看起来是帮助有需要的人的最好方式，特别是对少数民族和落后地区而言。透过行动和爱，我们能够帮助中国西南山区贫穷的少数民族，并且透过与他们合作而学习了很多。

我以前经常告诉我的队员，只要做你自己，自然地做盐和光，不用担心要宣道，只需要让我们的行动成为爱的信息。确实，不管我们到哪里宣道，我都可以很容易地想像耶稣在 2,000 年前会怎样做，在同样的村民和穷人中做一个高尚的楷模。

在我们开始国际医疗服务之前，有几年的时间，我其中一位良师、来自澳门的蓝牧师，去了中国南部建立学校和做慈善事业。在 1980 年代，他是在中国以外走进去的第一批人。不管他走到哪里，

I used to tell our team members, just be yourself, be salt and light naturally, don't worry about preaching, just let our actions be the message of love. Indeed, wherever we went on our mission, I could imagine easily what Jesus might have been doing, 2,000 years earlier, among similar villagers and poor people, as a supreme role model.

For several years before we began MSI, one of my best teachers was Rev Lam of Macau who had been one of the first people from outside China, in the 1980s, to go into southern China, to set up schools and do charitable work. Wherever he went, he was respected and welcomed. He brought in our first medical team, in 1989, to go into villages in southern China, probably one of the first medical teams to do so during that opening era.

Rev Lam reminded us that most people in the villages had never even met a follower of Jesus, and did not know anything about Him. He thought that, doctors and nurses would be especially great as "salt and light." We were just to do the things that came naturally to us, medical and nursing care, without doing anything artificial, with lots of love, and making lots of friends! I thought this was just perfect, salt and light as it should be, nothing contrived or forced!

I think that, in America and in many affluent parts of the world, we have often forgotten the simple salt and light instruction of Jesus. Sometimes it seems we have even forgotten why we are here on earth. We just try to enjoy ourselves, with more money, more entertainment, more food, more cruises. There seems to be no end to all our "vanity of vanities" that King Solomon lamented in his later life. In many instances we have more vanities than even the great king experienced. Seeing all of our lives, thousands of years later, I can imagine him shaking his head sadly. We could say we have often lost our salt and our light.

However, instead of losing our salt and light, I can imagine many ways to restore it, even in affluent America. For example, one way is, let's go out and invite someone we don't know that well, for coffee, for lunch, for ice cream, just so that we can chat and have good relationships. A younger person; an

11. 盐和光
11. Salt and Light

他都受到尊敬和欢迎。他在 1989 年带领我们的第一个医疗团队来到南方的乡村,可能是改革开放以来第一个这样做的医疗队伍。

蓝牧师提醒我们,在村庄里大多数人从来没有遇见过耶稣的跟随者,也一点都不知道关于耶稣的事。他想,医生和护士刚好能够做"盐和光"。我们就自然而然地充满爱心地做我们该做的医疗和护理,没有任何做作,结交朋友!我想这也最好,盐和光就像它们本身一样,不需要加以筹画和强迫!

我觉得,在美国和世界许多富有的地方,我们经常忘记来自耶稣的这个简单的盐和光的教导。有些时候看起来我们甚至忘记了我们为什么来到世上。我们只想自己享受,赚更多的钱,更多娱乐,更多食物,更多豪华遊轮旅程。所罗门国王在晚年所感叹的"一切都是虚空",看起来在今世也没有尽头。很多时候我们甚至比伟大的国王所经历的虚空还多。我可以想像若他看见几千年后我们的生活,他会伤心摇头。可以说我们经常都失去我们的盐和光。

可是,我可以想像,即使在富裕的美国,也有很多办法去把盐和光找回来,不致失去。举个例子,一个方法是走出家门和我们不太熟悉的人去喝咖啡,吃午饭,吃霜淇淋,一起聊天和建立友谊。对方可以是年轻人、老年人、家人不在身边的人。我们遇见的每个人几乎都可以是一个机会,让我们这样去做盐和光。我们只需要聆听,我们可以愉快地聊天,能帮上忙的方法就会自然冒出来。

在一个大教会的前厅喝咖啡聊天。我喜欢做"游说者",和我一起聊天的人照自拍,特别是我能把我的书送人。盐、光和咖啡。
Just chatting over coffee in lobby of large church. I like the role of "lobbyist," taking selfies with those I chat with, especially if I can give away my coffee book. Salt, light and coffee.

old person; a person away from home. Practically anyone we meet can be an opportunity for this kind of salt and light. We can just listen, we can literally just chat merrily away, and ways to be helpful will naturally emerge.

Nearly always, by chatting face to face, we will experience a good feeling, a feeling of relationship, a feeling of better understanding, a feeling of common humanity. We will see, and realize that this is another individual that God loves, no matter what the background, culture, or even language. Yes of course it might cost a bit of money, but what are we keeping all that money for, anyway? We might even make a few new friends, and that would be priceless.

We had the greatest fun in Cincinnati to chat with hundreds of scholars from China, in so-called "English corners" that were spread out at the main cafeteria of the Children's Hospital. We just used the booths and tables to meet one on one, or one with 2-3 scholars, mostly just to help improve their verbal English skills. We learned so much, and made so many friends, simply by *chatting* in our primary language, which was English! How difficult can that be? And yet we were able to be helpful, encouraging, and stimulating to our friends, and we learned to appreciate many new cultural perspectives from these wonderful interactions. Salt and light to them, and some sort of salt and light to us, a secondary blessing.

Many people know my enthusiasm for bringing young people on short-term missions. A major reason is simply that this is one of the greatest impetuses for salt and light *training*. When we go out to another country (and the farther you go the better it is, I think), you are out of your comfort box, but suddenly you realize that *you* are indeed now *the* salt and light, a key part of the mission. So practically instantaneously, you begin to be more friendly, more communicative, more lively.

Because of the *strange* situation that you are in, on a mission field, surprisingly, you feel less constrained by normal rules, and thus *freer* about sharing your life and faith. And so you do that, just naturally and without any fanfare; ergo, you have naturally become salt and light. This is a subtle

11. 盐和光
11. Salt and Light

几乎每一次面对面的交谈，都会让我们有良好的感觉，感受到友情、更多的谅解、共同的人性。我们会看到和意识到另外一个人也是上帝所喜爱的，不论背景、文化，甚至语言。这当然会花一些钱，可是我们存钱要干什么呢？我们甚至可能结交到几个新朋友，这才是无价的。

我们在辛辛那提最大的乐趣就是和来自中国的几百个访问学者，在儿童医院的餐厅里的所谓"英语角"聊天。我们每桌一对一或一对两三个学者，主要都是帮助他们提高英语水准。只是用我们的母语，就是英语*聊天*，我们就学到了很多，也交了很多的朋友！这有多难呢？可是，我们还能够帮助、鼓舞，和激励我们的朋友，我们也从这些美妙的交谈中学到很多新的文化观点。对于他们，我们是盐和光，同时我们也得到来自盐和光的另外一层祝福。

许多人知道我有带年轻人去短宣的热忱。一个主要的原因就是来自盐和光*训练*的激励。当我们去别的国家（我觉得越远越好），你就需要离开你的安逸区，可是突然你会意识到*你*真的变成了*那*盐和光，成为了队伍里不可或缺的一员。所以你几乎立刻开始变得更友善，更爱交流，更活泼。

在外宣的工场，因为所处的*陌生*环境，你会意外地觉得不那么被常规束缚，因此*更容易*与人分享你的生命历程和信仰。你这样做，自然而不吹嘘的话，你就自然做了盐和光。这是一个微小却很好的训练，可以让你认识到你*甚至*在自己本土上也能做到！真的，你可以！

我们都知道最好的学习方法是在真实生活中、在行动中亲眼目睹地去学，这也是在短宣的过程中经常发生的情况。你看到宣道士行动，你看到队长行动，你看到队员行动，突然间你会发现你也能

great training that makes you realize, you could do this *even* back in the home country! And indeed, you can!

We all know that the best way to learn is to see something happening before our eyes, to see it in real life, to see it in action, and that's what usually happens on the short-term mission. You see the missionaries in action, you see your leaders in action, you see your team members in action, and suddenly you realize that you can do it also. *Role modeling is much more powerful* than lecturing. Being inspired, being touched, can give you motivation for life!

And suddenly, we realize that all the gifts that God has given to us, can be used as part of the salt and light mission that we are involved in. No matter whether it is music (even invite them to a musical event), art (draw them a picture), writing (send them a nice note), or just chatting, we can use all of that as salt and light to those around us. We realize quickly that, by giving of ourselves to others, basically what is meant by salt and light, we reduce our emphasis on ourselves, and the need to *expect* things from other people. Instead, we see how blessed it is *to give* of ourselves, in all kinds of situations!

During my busiest days in Cincinnati in my last decade there, I could literally be meeting someone for lunch every day. Lunchtime is such a great time for chatting, since people might be able to take off for an hour from work, and they are nearly always more relaxed during a meal. But certainly, afternoon coffee or ice cream times, depending on the age of the individual, are just as fun. It is the opportunity for one-on-one chats in a quiet relaxed place that is the key, where the magic of relationships, of salt and light, just happens!

In my later recent life, I think that the fact that an older more mature person would sit down and listen to someone younger for an hour, can likely itself be inspirational, and a very subtle form of salt and light. At least I think that's why younger people seem to be receptive. It's the role model effect, before their eyes, even a subtle "body language" effect, demonstrating love and concern.

做到。*榜样的力量远远胜过*说教。被激励，被感动，能带给你生活的动力！

突然间，我们发现上帝赐给我们的所有恩赐，都能用于我们参与的盐和光的使命。不管是音乐（甚至邀请别人去音乐会）、艺术（给别人画画）、写作（给别人写一张温暖的便条），或者只是聊天，我们都能使用，作为我们身边的人的盐和光。我们很快会意识到，当我们为别人付出的时候，就是所谓的做盐和光，我们减少了对自己的关注，和*期待*从别人那里收取的需要。相反，我们看到了在所有时候都把自己*摆上*，是多大的福气！

在我住在辛辛那提的最后十年最忙的时候，我真的能每天和人吃午饭。午餐时间是聊天的好时机，因为对方可以从工作中挤出一个小时，而且在吃饭的时候总是可以更放松。但是下午的咖啡或是霜淇淋小休时间，按个人的年龄而定，也一样有趣。关键是在一个安静放松的地方有一对一聊天的机会，人际关系以及盐和光的奇妙作用就在这时出现了！

盐、光和中国菜，出现在我们常去的餐馆。
Salt, light and Chinese food, at a favorite place.

We are clearly affected by everything that happens around us. If the one third of the world which is Christian, would live a life that is salt and light, the world would be vastly different, and changed for the better. And those who show the salt and light will be hugely impacted themselves, their lives clearly becoming more meaningful and "abundant," just like the John 10:10 declaration.

And, there are indeed thousands of ways you could be salt and light. Practically anything, any personal gift or talent you have, can become salt and light. Just give it some thought and prayer, and let your creative juices help inspire you. And go!

盐、光和电脑没出故障时的视频聊天。
Salt, light and video chats when the computer doesn't freeze.

11. 盐和光
11. *Salt and Light*

在我最近的生活中，我认为一个年长、更成熟的人愿意坐下来听一个较年轻的人讲一个小时，本身就很令人振奋，而这也是做盐和光的一种微妙的方式。至少我觉得这是较年轻的人看起来容易受教的原因。这是榜样的力量，出现在他们面前，甚至是某种"肢体语言"的效果，表达着爱和关心。

我们明显地被我们身边发生的事情影响着。如果世界上三分之一的人，也就是基督徒，都愿意过盐和光的生活，世界会截然不同，变得更美好。那些展现出盐和光的人也会大受影响，他们的生活显然变得更有意义和"丰盛"，就像约翰福音十章 10 节宣告的一样。

你可以有千万个方式去做盐和光。几乎是你拥有的任何东西、任何个人的恩赐或才能，都能做盐和光。花一些时间想一想和祷告，让你的创作力帮助你。去做吧！

翻译：Dan Zhao、Aiden Zhao

12. Evangelism as Mission: the CCC Story

O ur church (Cincinnati Chinese Church) began from a bible study fellowship, active in outreach and evangelism on the college campus. This was likely similar to stories of a number of Chinese churches during the 1960s and 1970s, especially in smaller Midwest cities. There were few established Chinese churches in the Midwest, but Chinese bible study groups seemed to be on every college campus. Many of these bible study groups morphed into churches under so-called "lay leadership". Counterintuitively, they were often *unattached* to any particular denomination or larger church system, and were not necessarily "started" by ministers or pastors. Later on, and especially in large cities with significant Asian populations, minister-started churches were increasingly prevalent. But for us at the time, it seemed truly like a Spirit-led "natural gestation", leading from bible study group to the "natural birth" of our church. For a neonatologist specializing in newborn babies, it seemed pretty normal to me!

As a bible study fellowship, we mobilized nearly everyone in our group to visit the university campus on a weekly basis. It was really a heady time, meeting many overseas students and getting good responses, when at the same time our new church was being planned and started. We could sense that it was truly a "historic" time, and we were all quite excited.

Weekly, a team of ten or so got together on campus on Saturday evening and prayed for thirty minutes about the visits that night. Then we went out, two by two, just as advised in the Bible, to visit those we had

12. 以传福音为使命：
辛城教会的故事

我们的教会（辛城教会）起源于在大学校园里接触社群和传福音的查经团契。这个故事可能和不少 1960 和 1970 年代建立的华人教会相似，特别是那些在中西部小城里的教会。那时候中西部正式的华人教会十分罕见，不过多数大学校园里似乎都有中文查经团契。这些查经团契在会友（平信徒）领袖的带领下，很多都成长成为教会。很特别的是，这些教会通常都*不属于*任何支派或者较大的教会组织，也不一定是由传道人或者牧师"建立"。那种由牧师建立的教会在后来，特别是在有众多华人的大城市里，逐渐普遍起来。但是对当时的我们来说，我们的教会真的就像由圣灵"孕育"、从查经小组"自然出生"的教会。对作为新生儿科医生的我来说，这像是最自然不过的！

作为一个查经团契，我们每周都动员组里几乎每一个成员到校园里。那是一个令人振奋的时期，我们接触到许多留学生，得到很好的回响，同一时间我们也计画成立我们的教会。我们对这个"历史性"的时刻都无比兴奋。

每一周我们大概十个人在周六傍晚到校园里为当晚的访谈祷告 30 分钟。之后我们就如圣经上所说的，两个人一组去探访那些我们在周三或周四联络过的学生。我们奉耶稣之名去见各式各样的

contacted the prior Wednesday or Thursday. It was really quite simple, and very heartwarming, to be able to go out in the name of Jesus, to meet all kinds of people, and to share the wonderful good news. When the outreach became more "established", we tried to have about six sessions of training for newcomers before going out, but the most important training was still essentially *on-the-job* training.

Every time, by going out, in twos or threes, we were able to encourage each other, and the less experienced members were also able to watch and learn from the more senior persons. I vividly remember Pastor John Whitcomb (author of *The Genesis Flood*) telling us about his youthful enthusiasm during his *first* evangelism visit: he was eager and well prepared to debate with anyone he met. His first visit included a man who clearly did not want to be visited and slammed the door after making a sweeping comment that he could not believe "Jonah and the whale".

John was eager to take him on, but his senior colleague gently brushed John aside. John's colleague knocked on the door again, and politely asked the man for a few minutes of his time in order to simply present the main essence of the Gospel, and then *afterwards* to talk about Jonah. To John's surprise, the man agreed, and not that many minutes later, to John's further amazement, he gave his life to Jesus. When John asked the man, "What about Jonah and the big fish?" (it wasn't necessarily a whale), the man said, "Somehow, that doesn't seem to matter anymore." Instead of a fruitless debate about Jonah and the great fish, the man had come to Jesus, which was clearly the important reason for the visit!

John often liked to say, "You could win the battle (argue and win the Jonah story), but lose the war (the reason for the visit)!" Far better to do things politely, step by step, and no need to get into unnecessary confrontations! There's even a bible verse that says just that, 1 Peter 3:15: "Always be ready to give an answer to everyone who asks you for a reason regarding the hope that is in you, yet answer with *gentleness and reverence*."

Nowadays, there are many manuals teaching us how to go out and

人，和他们分享福音——很简单的行动，也很窝心。在我们的探访比较"有规模"之后，我们开始在新人出去探访之前为他们上六堂课，不过最重要的课还是实际的*在职*培训。

每一次我们以两人或三人一组的形式去探访，我们都互相鼓励，而经验较少的组员可以观察并从经验较多的组员身上学习。我很清楚记得约翰·惠特科姆牧师（《创世记中的洪水》的作者）对我们谈到他带着初生之犊的精神*第一次*去传福音的情形。他准备充足并愿意和任何人辩论。他遇到了一个明显不愿意被他探访的人，那人以偏概全地指出他不能相信"约拿和鲸鱼"之后就用力把门关上。

早期的探访同工。他们当时也是初信主，现在已积极地服事密西西比州学生以及学者探访事工。

Early outreach visitors who were new believers themselves, now actively engaged in outreach to students and scholars in Mississippi.

约翰想正面与他辩论，不过比他有经验的队友阻止了他。他的队友又敲了门，并很有礼貌地问那个人是否有几分钟的时间让他陈述福音的精髓，*之后*再来谈约拿。出乎约翰意料之外，那个人居然答应了。更让约翰难以置信的是，不久之后，那人居然把他的生命交给了耶稣。约翰问他"你不是对约拿和大鱼还有疑问吗？"（那条大鱼并不一定是鲸鱼）那人回答说："那个已经不重要了。"结果没有无谓地为约拿和大鱼争论，而是那人来到了耶稣面前。这才是他们去探访最重要的原因！

约翰常常喜欢说："你可能赢了一场战役（辩赢了约拿的故

witness...but in those days, 50 years ago, many of these were still quite novel. Because of that, we had many opportunities to devise our *own* system. For example, nowadays, Evangelism Explosion is well established and copyrighted, but then it was just beginning, so we could modify some of the principles for our own cultural or cross-cultural needs, and I think "our system" seemed to be just as helpful. Especially as we combined it with other approaches, such as the principles of Campus Crusade's Four Spiritual Laws and the so-called "Roman way". We even later printed our own practical booklet in Taiwan, in Chinese, simply called "Visitation".

Anyway, the fun of training, calling the potential person to be visited ahead of time, praying before the start of the visit, and experiencing the actual visit were all part of the joy and excitement of seeing many come to know the message of love! We learned so much by doing, and clearly, if we didn't go, we would not have learnt!

No evangelism means a dead church. No evangelism means no life. During the evangelism visits we could sense the Lord with us at all points. It was just amazing. These visits were part of making everyone at the church a natural evangelist. It was great to see that, step by step, indeed, evangelism truly became our developing church's lifeblood. After all, it is the *good news*: "gospel" is *literally* "good news" in Greek, and in a wonderful way, in Chinese it is also simply and clearly *fu (good) yin (news)*, 福音 , *good news*, the news of a new life, the news of eternal life. What better lifeblood message could we be bringing?

The key was to go, go, go. We encouraged everyone to move out of their comfort zone, to be concerned for others, to help others, *to be the fuyin.* Sometimes people just tagged along, but that was just fine, because it was such a good learning experience for them. Learning on the job is truly one of the best ways to learn. It's role modeling, it's apprenticeship, it's mentoring on the go.

We would often debrief quickly at the end of the visit, either in the car in twos or threes, or at some central meeting point for the evening's team, when

事），但输了整个战争（探访的原因）！"我们不需要无谓的对质。有礼貌、一步一步地做事才是更好的方法。圣经正好有一节经文告诉我们这个道理。彼得前书三章 15 节："有人问你们心中盼望的缘由，就要常作准备，以*温柔、敬畏的心*回答各人。"

今天有许多书本教导我们如何走出去作见证……但是在 50 年前这些都还是很新的概念。因此我们有很多机会设计我们*自己*作见证的方式。例如，三元福音在今天已是根深蒂固，受到版权保护。不过在当时三元福音才刚起步，因此我们可以针对我们文化或跨文化上的需要做一些调整。我觉得"我们的方式"也好像一样有效，特别是我们把它和其他的方法，例如是学园传道会的四个属灵定律和所谓的"罗马道路"结合在一起时，更适合我们。我们后来更在台湾用中文印制了我们自己的实用手册，简单地称为《探访》。

有趣的培训，事先联络那些我们想要探访的人，在探访前祷告，探访过程的经历，以及见到许多人认识了爱的信息，全都让我们满心喜乐振奋！我们在实践中学到太多，这些事我们若不亲自去做就不可能学到！

不传福音的教会是死的。不传福音就没有生命。每当我们出去传福音，我们都能感觉到主全程与我们同在。那真的很奇妙。这些探访让教会里的每一个人自然而然地成了传道者。我们很欣慰地见到传福音成为我们成长中的教会的生命泉源。追根究底，福音就是*好消息*："福音"在希腊文中的*字面意思*就是"好消息"，而中文"福（好）音（消息）"比英文的 gospel 更清楚地表达了这个有关新生命的消息，一个有关永生的消息。除此以外，我们还能带给人更好的有关生命泉源的信息吗？

关键是不断地出去。我们鼓励所有人走出自己的舒适圈，关心

we could review the highlights of the evening's visits, depending on how late it was. That was always a great time to recap what had happened and to learn from each experience. It seemed we were experiencing a spiritual high weekly, and truly what a meaningful high!

加州受探访事工激励的年轻弟兄姐妹。Ken 后来成为洛杉矶一间大教会里的忠心执事。

Young California believers, inspired by going on outreach visits; Ken later became an active deacon in a large Los Angeles church.

I can remember many names of wonderful "visitation workers", among them Ivy, Gan, Chip, Meichi, John, Ken, Jiayang, David, Daniel, James, Mary, and leaders Shipei and Elaine, faithful people who continued to serve in many different cities all over the world. Some have indicated that these visitations were what started them on their lifelong journey of personal testimonies everywhere, kind of like the effect of training programs that we later instituted for overseas short-term missions. Both are similarly great preparations for all of life!

There are many methods of outreach evangelism, and each person learns how to do it with their own creativity, given the different circumstances and personalities involved. One of the more interesting approaches, and a very touching one, was the later outreach to restaurant-related people. Chinese restaurant workers are always so busy, and they usually don't finish their daily work until 10 p.m., which is a totally different schedule from the lives of most other people.

So, David, our pastor, took the creative step of going to the restaurants *after 10 p.m.*, starting bible study groups right then and there, or giving evangelism talks, and generally making friends with a neglected population. Soon, many people joined him in these outreach efforts, and at one time there were like five different restaurant-related bible study groups all over the Cincinnati/Northern Kentucky region. Encouragingly, the children of the restaurant workers are now growing up in Sunday School, and have truly

他人，帮助他人，*让自己成为福音*。有时候一些人只是跟着我们去传福音，这并没有问题，因为这些都是很好的学习机会。在实践中学习是最好的学习方法。这是以身作则，学徒培训，行为指导的教学。

若时间允许，探访结束后我们通常会聚在一起，或是两三个人在车里，或是当时全体队员在一个聚集点，简短讨论当晚探访的重点。回顾所发生的事总是让我们彼此学到很多东西。我们每周都好像经历着属灵的高点，一个真正有意义的高点！

我仍记得许多有恩赐的"探访同工"，像是 Ivy、Gan、Chip、Meichi、John、Ken、Jiayang、David、Daniel、James、Mary，和负责带领的斯白和依南。这些忠心的同工之后去到许多国家城市继续服事。他们一些人指出那些早期的探访经历，启发他们在世界各地展开持续一生的个人见证之旅。这跟我们后来为海外短宣设立的训练课程有着异曲同工的效果。两者同样有效地为我们的人生作好装备。

对外传福音有很多种方法。我们通过学习和创意来找出这些因人而异也因地而异的方法。我们后来向餐饮业工作人员传福音，就是其中一个比较特别也触动人心的方法。中餐馆的工作人员四季忙碌，每日工作至晚上 10 时。他们有着跟大多数人完全不一样的日常生活。

因此，我们的牧师吴继扬采取了有创意的第一步，在*晚上 10时后*到餐馆里开始查经小组，或在那里讲福音信息，和这些被忽略的人建立友谊。不久，许多人加入了这个事工。有一段时间我们在辛辛那提和北肯塔基一带有五个不同的餐馆查经小组。令人振奋的是，这些餐馆工作人员的子女现时就在我们的儿童主日学里成长，

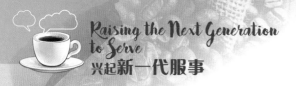
become the exciting next generation to serve the Lord. A wonderful testimony indeed.

One thing always very touching about Chinese churches actively engaged in evangelism outreach is that there are many immersion baptisms. Often an Easter baptism service, as well as a fall baptism service. At times it seemed there were like 50 baptisms a year in our church, which steadily grew to 500, even despite a high turnover rate because of the large student population, who often moved on after school, as well as tendency of families to move to bigger coastal cities.

Without any doubt, a key factor in all of this is that non-Christians have to see Christians in real life, and not just inside a church building. Especially for overseas students and scholars. We can be very practical and helpful to them in many ways, helping them go through the difficulties of adjusting to the new culture, sorting out living arrangements, getting driver licenses, solving banking issues, and even language learning. By inviting them to dinner, just meeting and chatting with them, we can find many opportunities to love them as Jesus would love them. *Showing them* the love of Jesus is unquestionably "louder" than just talking about it! Just go for it!

And welcome them at some point to church at great times like Welcome New Students Party, Thanksgiving, Christmas, Chinese New Year and Easter. As a church, we actually began to use all five of these occasions creatively, to have dinners and evangelistic talks, often including a quality music program, skits or testimonies to make the evening interesting and lively. People need to see the whole church together, worshiping together, and experiencing a corporate joy that they may not find elsewhere.

There are lots of feelings of emptiness all over the world, a sense of meaninglessness, which the message of love can overcome. And in our context, it doesn't hurt that our Chinese friends love to congregate where there is a crowd that is excited and exciting, where there is great *renau* (the *not* translatable Chinese word for festivity, noise and lots of people)! Church *renau*! All this is especially important in the context of always being salt and

真真正正成为要服事主的下一代。这是一个很美妙的见证。

对于积极参与向外传福音的华人教会来说，看到许多人接受浸礼总是让人觉得无比感动。我们通常有一个复活节浸礼和一个秋季浸礼。有一段时间，我们教会一年里大概有 50 个人接受浸礼。我们教会人口流动频繁，因为很多学生毕业后离开辛城，也有家庭举家搬到东西岸较大的城市，但即便如此，教会人数仍逐渐增加到 500 多人。

其中一个关键因素无疑就是让非基督徒不仅在教会内、更在教会以外的日常生活里接触到基督徒。特别是对海外学生或学者，我们可以给他们很多种实质上的帮助，例

向中餐馆员工传福音，结果建立了餐馆查经小组。来自不同餐馆的员工也有了愉快的交流。
Evangelism to Chinese restaurant staff results in restaurant bible study groups and delightful interactions among restaurants.

如帮助他们适应当地文化，解答日常起居的问题，考取驾照，银行开户，或者学习语言。邀请他们一起吃晚饭或者见面聊天，就可以找到很多机会关怀他们，传达耶稣的爱。*让他们*从我们的行动中*看到*耶稣的爱，比仅仅在口头上说耶稣的爱"更有力"。去做就对了！

不要忘记在特别节庆时，例如新生欢迎会、感恩节、圣诞节、春节和复活节，邀请他们来教会。我们的教会就在这五个节庆里有创意地预备晚饭、福音讲道、音乐节目、短剧或见证，让晚会生动有趣。人们需要看见整个教会如同一个肢体在一起崇拜，并感觉到别处没有的合一的喜乐。

light, everywhere, at all times. See chapter 11 "Salt and Light".

Let me conclude with a little story. I was driving around the University campus, and noticed a distraught young woman, obviously from overseas, walking on the streets looking confused and sad. Years later, she recounted often that the phrase, "How can I help you?" was such a wonderful relief to her, and pretty soon we were having a light meal, and helping her find an apartment. Of course, she came to church after that, and the rest is history. Nowadays she is very active in ministry and helping many young people herself.

She loves to tell this story of how she became a believer, and yet it is a story that could happen every day, if we would just remember to ask the simple question, "How can I help you?" Indeed, do that and you will be amazed how many doors will be opened, and how many lives will be touched!

I think all this reflects that evangelism truly is the blood of the church, and the clear realization is that there are so many evangelism opportunities staring us in the face. Especially if we put our heads together, to think and plan creatively, as we pray for guidance for the right approaches. We should never waste these great opportunities! Go for it!

当年失落于校园走道上的年轻海外学生如今热心参与年轻留学生的事工。这类故事我们很多人都亲身经历过。

Young overseas student, "found lost on the pavement of University campus", now involved in active ministry to overseas young students. A story maybe many can identify with.

爱的信息可以战胜这个世界的空洞和空虚。我们华人朋友们在碰到有趣或者值得庆祝的事情时，喜欢招朋引友在一起聚会，图个*热闹*。因此，我们随时随地都能在人群里作盐作光，就更是重要了。请参看本书第 11 章"盐和光"。

我用一个小故事来做结尾。有一天我在辛城大学校园里开车，我注意到一位明显是来自海外的年轻女士，她看起来十分焦虑，困惑、难过地在路上走着。多年后她还常常忆述当时的一句"有什么需要帮忙吗？"让她如释重担。不久，我就和她一起吃了个简餐，并帮助她找到一间公寓居住。后来她很自然地也就来到我们的教会了。今天她非常积极地事奉，也亲自帮助了许多年轻人。

她喜欢和别人分享她信主的经历。只要我们记得简单地问一句"有什么需要帮忙吗？"，她的经历每天都有可能发生。你只要去做，就会很惊奇地发现上帝将打开许多扇门，很多生命将因你而改变！

我想这些事都显明了传福音真的是教会的血脉，而且我们每天都会遇到许多传福音的机会。我们应该集思广益，在思路上和计画上创新，并且为合适的福音传播方式祷告求上帝引领。我们绝对不该枉费这些美好的机会！让我们一起去做！

翻译：Edison

13. Decisions, Decisions, Decisions I: There Is a Model

Decisions, decisions, decisions. They seem to be the problem that causes most confusion and disagreements in a church. There is a *not-so-nice joke* that Asian churches have too many "big heads," "too many PhD's," too many people who are doing quite well in secular professions, who bring secular decision-making approaches *into the church*. In curiosity, I looked around one time during a church committee meeting, and was surprised that indeed, about half of the members were PhDs, which sounds quite weird, as if we were in a college campus. I guess it is so common we don't really even pay any attention to it.

There is also a rumor that splits in Asian churches are quite common, and usually related to unhappiness with church decisions. Whether this is true or not, I'm not totally sure, but I certainly know of many splits that occurred in cities near us, seemingly like practically every Chinese speaking church, so we know that definitely there are many problems that we should pay attention to, big heads or not.

One misunderstanding is indeed common: many Asians, or maybe even average Americans, unconsciously, simply think that churches are like USA society, a *democracy*. Many have migrated here to a "free society" that was born of "Christian principles," so therefore they think they can just bring in some of the ways of US society into their churches also, assuming *somehow*

13. 决定、决定、决定（一）：
有一个模式

决定，决定，决定。这似乎是造成教会混乱和分歧最多的问题。有一个*不太好的笑话*，指亚裔教会有太多"大人物"，"太多博士"，太多在世俗职业中表现非常出色的人，将世俗的决策方法*带入教会*。出于好奇，一次我在教会委员会会议期间环顾过，令我感到惊讶的是，其中确实有大约一半的成员是博士，这情况听起来很奇怪，好像我们正身处大学校园一样。我估计这情况很常见，所以我们甚至都没有注意到它。

还有传言说在亚裔教会中，分裂是相当普遍的，并且通常是与不满教会的决定有关。我不完全确定这是否事实，但我当然听说过我们附近城市有很多教会出现分裂，看起来像是几乎每间华语教会都是这样，所以我们知道肯定有很多问题需要注意，不管教会中有没有大人物。

有一种误解确实是很普遍：许多亚洲人，或者甚至是普通美国人，不知不觉地认为教会就像美国社会一样是个*民主制度*。很多亚洲人移民来到了一个以基督教原则为根基的"自由社会"。所以，他们认为他们也可以将美国社会的一些方式带入他们的教会，假设这些也*差不多*是基督教原则。例如，一个简单的逻辑就是：在一个民主的制度下，我们要投票，所以在教会中我们也理所当然地以投

that these are Christian principles. For example, a simple logic is, of course, we vote in a democracy, so in church we will simply vote and decide on issues, just like US elections, which "somehow" relate to the Christian foundations of our society.

And, yet, on simple reflection, we know how complicated, unsatisfactory, and frankly chaotic, US elections are! Definitely, it is *not a good model* for church decisions. And, surprise, it is definitely *not* biblical! The biblical model for church management is, to be emphatic, actually *not* democracy! And that's one of the first *myths* we should dispel.

Acts 13:1-4 (NIV): "Now in the church at Antioch there were prophets and teachers: Barnabas, Simeon called Niger, Lucius of Cyrene, Manaen (who had been brought up with Herod the tetrarch) and Saul. While they were worshiping the

Lord and fasting, the Holy Spirit said, 'Set apart for me Barnabas and Saul for the work to which I have called them.' So after they had fasted and prayed, they placed their hands on them and sent them off. The two of them, sent on their way by the Holy Spirit, went down to Seleucia and sailed from there to Cyprus. "

In fact, to possibly some people's great surprise, the basic driving principle of church management, according to the Bible, is to simply *seriously seek God's will*. In this passage, the leadership group of prophets and teachers worshipped, fasted and prayed, and were guided by the Spirit of God in their decision.

第一间教会的重大决定、决定、决定：在不同时间差派他们的重要领导者保罗，这肯定是一个心痛的决定。图片取自谷歌安全搜索。

First church major decision, decision, decision, to send away, at different times, their great leader Paul, which must have been a heart-wrenching decision.

https://upload.wikimedia.org/wikipedia/commons/e/ee/Bartolomeo_Montagna_-_Saint_Paul_-_Google_Art_Project.jpg. Google safe search, all uses.

票来做决定，解决问题，就像美国的选举一样，它"某种程度上"与我们社会的基督教基础有关。

然而，简单想想我们就知道，美国的选举是多么复杂，令人不满意，坦率地说是多么混乱！这肯定*不是*教会做决定的*好榜样*。而且，令人惊讶的是，这绝对也*不符合圣经原则*！要强调：教会管理的圣经模式实际上*不是*民主制度！这是我们应该首先消除的其中一个谬见。

使徒行传十三章 1 至 4 节："在安提阿的教会中，有几位先知和教师，就是巴拿巴和称呼尼结的西面、古利奈人路求，与分封之王希律同养的马念，并扫罗。他们事奉主、禁食的时候，圣灵说：'要为我分派巴拿巴和扫罗，去做我召他们所做的工。'于是禁食祷告，按手在他们头上，就打发他们去了。他们既被圣灵差遣，就下到西流基，从那里坐船往赛浦路斯去。"

事实上，可能让很多人惊讶的是，根据圣经，教会管理的基本驱动原则，只是*认真地寻求上帝的旨意*。在这段经文中，作为教会领导团队的先知和教师集体崇拜、禁食和祷告，并在圣灵的指导下做出决定。决定总是集体决定；例如长老总是有*多位*，决不会由一位"独裁者"式的牧师作出决定。在圣经中，长老和牧师是相同的，但现在牧师通常由教会提供财政支援，而长老一般除了服事教会外，还有其他职业。

实际上，教会*领导*的主要责任是寻求上帝的旨意。这听起来很古老，甚至很抽象，人们可能会认为这是不可能的！但我们是不是信一位无所不能的上帝呢？意思是，我认为上帝的方式不应"就像世界上自然发生的事情"，尤其是不像世俗世界，也不像西方世界。我们绝对应该首先遵循圣经原则，而不是"自然的方式"，也不是

And decisions were always group decisions; e.g. there were always a *plurality* of elders, and never a decision made alone by a "dictator" type of pastor. In the bible, elders and pastors are the same, though in today's usage pastors are usually financially supported by the church, whereas elders generally have a separate profession in addition to serving the church.

In effect, the *leadership* of the church is given the main responsibility to seek God's will. That sounds very ancient, and even very abstract, and people might think that that is impossible! But don't we believe that God is the God of the impossible? Meaning, I think God's ways are *not* meant to be "just like what happens naturally in the world," especially not the secular world, nor the western world. We definitely should try to follow biblical principles first, and not the "natural way," nor the "American way."

Some people also like to say the Bible doesn't really lay out how a church is to run. Surprise! There are actually *lots of principles* in the Bible, about how to work with people, and how to deal with issues. And church management means we have to deal with people and issues. *So,* it's not true that we are just left to devise our own system without clear guidance. Plus, what about all those verses about *elders and deacons*, the key components of any church management. There certainly are a lot of descriptions of qualifications and responsibilities for them, and therefore the expectations for proper church management.

And, there is another *secret*, which is, even though titles of bible chapters don't say "How to organize a church," we actually even have a pretty detailed description of what happened to the *first church*. So, we can definitely learn from the practical example of the early church, and especially the letters from Paul, which especially often deal with *practical issues within the church*, so there is plenty of material to work with. It's just whether we want to follow them or not.

As a first step, I think therefore, every responsible person in the church should read how the early church managed its problems, as a *model*. The principles that derive from the early church are extremely instructive, even

"美国的方式"。

有些人也喜欢说圣经并没有真正展示教会应如何运作。意外的是，圣经中实际上有*很多原则*，论到如何与人合作以及如何处理问题。教会管理意味着我们必须与人和问题打交道。*所以*，我们不能说没有明确的指引而需要自己设计教会的体系。另外，还有关于*长老和执事*的所有经文呢？他们是教会管理的关键组成部分。圣经中当然有很多关于他们的资格和责任的描述，因此也是对恰当地管理教会的期望。

还有另外一个*秘诀*，就是尽管圣经章节的题目没有说"如何管理教会"，但对于*第一间教会*所发生的事，我们其实还是有非常详细的描述。所以，我们当然可以从早期教会的实际例子中学习，尤其是经常处理*教会中的实际问题*的保罗书信，给了我们很多材料可以参考。问题只是我们是否愿意效法。

因此我认为第一步，教会中的每个负责人都应该阅读了解早期教会如何处理它的问题，以此作为一个*榜样*。尽管那是 2,000 年前的事，但从早期教会衍生出来的原则是非常具有启发性的。或者我们应该说，*特别是因为它已有 2,000 年的历史*，一次又一次被试验和使用，所以是非常有价值的。就像宗教改革给我们的提醒那样，我们需要*回归*圣经，而不仅仅是遵循多年来在西方宗派结构中积累下来的传统。

记住教会是一个活的有机体，所以它不仅仅是理论和哲学。别以这个现代的节奏为借口，然后说："哦，圣经太古老了，我们可以相信它适用于现代社会和现代教会吗？"这种反应可能是今天教会中存在如此多问题的原因：我们*忘了*查看圣经从教会一开始就清楚告诉我们，我们能做什么，该做什么。

though it's 2,000 years ago. Or maybe we should say, it is so valuable *especially since it has a 2,000-year history* that has been tested and used, again and again. Just like we are all reminded from the Reformation, we need to go *back* to the Bible, and not just follow the traditions accumulated over the years in western denominational structure.

Remember the church is a living organism, so it is not just theory and philosophy. And don't give me this modern spin, and say, "O, the Bible is such an old book, can we trust it, for modern society and modern churches?" This response is probably why there are so many problems in today's churches: we *forgot* to check what the Good Book clearly told us we can and should do, from the very beginning of the church.

Traditions that have been started, and added down the centuries are interesting, and may be helpful, especially during *their* culture and time, but these traditions may not be the most helpful for our specific church. Better to check with the *original* and go from there, as the "main frame," taking some other traditions that have come along if they could be helpful or needed, as "add-ons," instead of vice versa.

Read Acts 15 especially carefully please. In this chapter there is a detailed example of how the early church dealt with a controversial issue about the gentiles' salvation. The leaders did not focus on advantages or disadvantages, like we commonly do, or what the majority wanted, or even what was best for the gentiles. They did *not* vote. And the leaders were given the responsibility to make the main decision. From principles that are clearly in the scriptures, and personal experience, here are some guiding thoughts, that should help us in making decisions for our "modern" church, using these "*case studies*" as a start.

1. Prayer

Prayer works! Again, you might think, of course, everyone says that, and anyway, that's too abstract and too theoretic! But in reality, that's the

已经开始并且延续了几个世纪的传统很有趣，也可能会有所帮助，尤其是在*它们的*文化和时期来说，但这些传统对我们特定的教会可能并不是最有帮助的。最好还是查看圣经这个*正本*，并从那里出发，用它作为"主要框架"，将其他可能有用或需要的传统作为"附件"，而不是本末倒置。

请仔细阅读使徒行传十五章。在这一章中，有一个关于早期教会如何处理外邦人救赎的争议问题的详细例子。教会的领导者没有像我们通常所做的那样把重点放在优点或缺点上，或是聚焦于多数人想要的是什么，甚或是对外邦人来说最好的是什么。他们*没有*投票。领导者有责任做出主要决定。根据圣经中明确的原则和个人经验，以下有一些指导性想法，应该能帮助我们为我们的"现代"教会作出决定。就以这些"*案例研究*"作为出发点吧。

1. 祷告

祷告能起作用！你可能又会想，当然，人人都这么说，反正这太抽象了，只是理论！但实际上，这是最好的方法。这是符合圣经的方法。它有 6,000 年的历史。它受到所有信徒的高度重视。而且，我并不是指在会议开始和 / 或结束时匆匆地作祝福的敷衍祈祷，就像"主啊，祝福我们*已经*做出的决定"。或者教会爱发出的典型"*盖章*式*祷告*"："主啊，请盖章同意！"这似乎不是最初的合乎圣经的"风格"。

从会议的*每个*成员的严肃祷告开始好吗？这样，每个人都有十足的权利来参与。真正花些时间祷告，专注于真诚地寻找上帝的旨意好吗？在讨论期间也祷告，间歇地、特别是当出现僵局时*停下来*

best way. It's biblical. It has a 6,000-year history. It is highly regarded by all believers. And, I don't mean the rather perfunctory prayer of quick blessing at the beginning and/or end of the meeting, like "Lord, bless us for a decision we have *already* made." Or, "Lord, just stamp OK," the typical *"rubber stamp prayer"* churches love. That doesn't seem to be the original biblical "style."

How about starting with serious prayer from *each* of the members of the meeting? That way, each person has a fully vested involvement. How about really spending some time praying and focusing on sincerely finding out God's will? How about keep on praying during the discussions, by *stopping and praying* intermittently and especially when there is an impasse. That is novel, and yet should not be novel, since it seems more consistent with *the Book*.

And reminding ourselves we should never say "there's not enough time to pray." If we ever say that, please stop!! And pray! One time, a senior member of the leadership said that, and instantly, everyone froze, since we all realized that something was indeed wrong. And seriously pray *just before* you are to make a decision, instead of *after* the decision!! You will find that, amazingly, it works. God helps us to direct our thoughts towards Him and what is His specific will in the subject at hand, and surprisingly we can come to some kind of better agreement for our decision.

If you still think that prayer is too abstract, I'll give you many good "side effects" that could encourage you. Haven't you always found that when you pray together, instantly you actually feel humbled, because you are praying to God! Your temper immediately changes, and you might even be quietly reminded to consider your fellow colleagues in a more gentle way! Which quite changes the dynamic, mainly because I think you're reminded that we are all focused on God, and therefore this is a serious matter, and not just an argument between 2 or 3 people!

The biggest practical reason God's will needs to be *prayerfully* sought, however, is Jesus *modeled* it dramatically Himself, in the historic "not my will" passage, the moment of His greatest decision, to commit His greatest act.

祷告。这是新颖的做法，但不应该是新颖的，因为它看起来更符合*圣经*。

　　提醒我们自己绝不应该说"我们没时间祷告"。如果我们这样说，请停止！并祷告！有一次，领导层一位资深的成员这样说，所有人马上呆住了，因为我们都意识到的确出了问题。并且在你*快要*做出决定*之前*认真地祷告，而不是等到下决定*之后*！你会发现，令人惊讶的是，这样做是有效的。上帝帮助我们把思想转向祂，明白祂对这个问题的具体旨意是什么，令人惊讶的是，我们这样就可以达成某种更好的决议。

耶稣在客西马尼园热切寻求上帝的旨意。即使祂是上帝的儿子也这样，我们怎么敢在教会做决定时不真心寻求上帝的旨意呢？图片取自谷歌安全搜索。

Jesus in the garden, fervently seeking God's will, even the Son of God, so how dare we not truly seek God's will in our church decisions? https://upload.wikimedia.org/wikipedia/commons/5/59/Painting_of_Christ_in_Gethsemane.jpg. Google safe search, all uses.

Matthew 26:39: "And He went a little beyond them, and fell on His face and prayed, saying, 'My Father, if it is possible, let this cup pass from Me; yet not as I will, but as You will.'" If the Lord Himself modeled it for us, who are we to doubt it?

Note that even for Jesus, He had to pray with tremendous fervor. He sought the will of God always, even when He knew it would mean His own struggle, anguish and death. He was submissive to the greater will of God and did not seek the easy way out, the simplest solution. So should we.

如果你仍然认为祷告太抽象了，我告诉你祷告有许多正面的"副作用"，这可能会鼓励你。难道你不是总会发现当你们一起祷告时，就会立刻谦卑下来吗？因为你在向上帝祈祷！你的脾气也会立即改变，你甚至可能会被悄悄提醒，以更温柔的方式考虑同工们的意见！这会改变当时的情况，我认为主要是因为祷告提醒你，我们都要聚焦于上帝，因此这是一件严正的事情，而不仅仅是两三个人之间的争论！

然而，要*祷告*寻求上帝的旨意的最大理由是，耶稣在"不要照我的意思"那段历史性经文中，在祂要做出最伟大的决定、要作出最伟大的行动的时刻，亲自为我们*做了榜样*。马太福音二十六章39节："他就稍往前走，俯伏在地，祷告说：'我父啊，倘若可行，求你叫这杯离开我。然而，*不要照我的意思，只要照你的意思*。'"主既然亲自为我们做了榜样，我们有什么资格质疑呢？

请注意，即使是耶稣也必须非常热切地祷告。祂始终追求上帝的旨意，即使祂知道这意味着自己要挣扎，面对痛苦和死亡。祂顺服上帝那更高的旨意，并没有寻求最省事的方法，最简单的解决方案。我们也应当如此。

翻译：Grace Liu

14. Decisions, Decisions, Decisions II: Spirit to Consensus

...And so we continue, from part 1

2. Holy Spirit

You have heard that when the first disciples got together "to form their church," they started with prayer. The Holy Spirit descended on them, changed them, and made them a totally new energetic group, to begin *the very first* church in the world! Wouldn't you like to form a church that way? Personally, I have had the privilege and opportunity to start many church related efforts in my life, including being acting minister 7 times! So I know well the deep meaning and joy of the first step in any venture. Imagine the first steps of building the *original* church. It was really special, setting the stage for 2,000 years of the life of the church. I don't really understand why Christians don't pay more attention to how it all actually began! Much more exciting than many other efforts in the church, I am sure!

And I really think the principles embodied in the first church are much better than any secular, or even church management "strategy" workshops you might learn. Indeed, the popular good management guru books (which I have read quite extensively) often overtly, or covertly, use biblical principles, so why not just start with the Bible ourselves. *Get it from the source*, and save

14. 决定、决定、决定（二）：
圣灵、合一

......续上文

2. 圣灵

你已经知道当最早期的门徒聚集一起"建立他们的教会"的时候，他们是以祷告开始。圣灵降到他们身上，改变他们，也让他们变成一个全新的充满力量的群体，开始世界上*第一间*教会！你不想以这样的方式建立一间教会吗？我个人有这样的福气和机会在建立教会方面付出一些努力，包括 7 次成为代任牧师！所以我很清楚在任何旅程中，迈出第一步有多深刻的意义和喜乐。想像一下建立*原始*教会的最初几步——它们真的很特别，为 2,000 年的教会生活奠定了基础。我真的不明白为什么基督徒不多加注意教会其实是如何开始的！我确信它比教会的其他工作更让人兴奋！

我真的认为第一间教会所体现的原则，比你从任何世俗甚至教会管理"战略"的讲座里可能学到的都要好得多。事实上，管理大师那些流行的好书（我已经非常广泛地阅读过）经常公开或暗中使用圣经原则，所以我们自己为什么不从圣经开始。*从源头学习它，并节省金钱*。

the money.

And, in the beginning of the historic church, who do you think were leading the church? Was it a management guru? Was it a seminary trained pastor? Was it the president and CEO of a big organization? Was it a PhD? You know the answer. It was just common people, and the leading light of the group was a fisherman who had never gone to college.

But he and his coworkers had all *lived with, and followed* the greatest leader for 3 years, hearing what he had taught, seeing him in action, and praying with him. Day in and day out, they had learned their lessons, and now in their time of need, in their time of prayer, He was no longer on earth, but the Holy Spirit descended upon them to give them a new mission in life. Isn't this a beautiful picture of how a church should run, and especially how it should start?

Living our daily lives serving the Lord, and trying to follow Jesus teachings, rather than the world, is a great start. And letting the Holy Spirit guide, instead of just following our own dreams and plans, or somehow using our former church experience, tradition or denomination as the foundation, would seem a lot more exciting, and consistently biblical to me. After all, the Holy Spirit is a real living God and moves in the lives of Christians of all generations, so why don't we allow Him the freedom to act on our thoughts and lives, instead of simply copying some formula from sources other than the Bible.

I have a feeling that, just as in the great diversity of gifts chapter in the New Testament, not only is each believer the recipient of unique gifts, each *individual church* should have the joy of uniqueness also. It would seem reasonable that the Spirit moves and gives us all unique *corporate church gifts*, and each church can be so different from another one, so that we can truly celebrate that wonderful diversity, among churches! And that is only possible because we have a living Holy Spirit who animates us, individually and corporately!

而且，在历史悠久的教会开始时，你认为谁领导教会？是管理大师吗？是一个受过神学院训练的牧师吗？是一个大型组织的总裁兼首席执行官吗？是博士吗？你是知道答案的。只是普通人，最初教会的主要领导者是一名从未上过大学的渔夫。

但他和他的同工都和最伟大的领导者*一起生活，并跟随*祂三年，听祂所讲的，看祂所做的，并和祂一起祷告。日复一日，他们学到了功课，现在在他们需要的时候，在他们祷告的时候，祂不再在地上了，但圣灵降到他们身上，给他们的生活一个全新的使命。这不就是教会应该如何运作，尤其是应该如何开始的一个美丽画面吗？

每一天事奉主，并试着跟从耶稣的教导，而不是跟从世界，就是一个很好的开始。不是仅仅跟从我们自己的梦想和计划，又用我们以前的教会经验、传统或宗派作为基础，而是让圣灵带领，对我来说更符合圣经，也更令人兴奋。说到底，圣灵是真正活着的上帝，在世世代代的基督徒生命中作工。既是这样，我们为什么不让祂在我们的思想和生活中自由动工，而是从圣经以外的地方把一些公式搬过来？

我有一种感觉：新约圣经里有一章讲到恩赐的多样性，但不仅每一个信徒是独特恩赐的接受者，而

第一间教会等待着圣灵的内住和感动。图片取自谷歌安全搜索。

First church awaiting the Holy Spirit's inflowing and touching. Google safe search, all uses. http://commons.wikimedia.org/wiki/File:Pentecost_(Kirillo-Belozersk).jpg

3. Consensus

And do you think that the early church made their decisions by 51% majority vote? 60%? 75%? What do you think? The scriptures show us they decided major decisions by *consensus*. Acts 15:22: *"Then it seemed good to the apostles and the elders, with the whole church...."* (English Standard Version)

Over the decades of the church we started, we have taken the concept of "*seemed good* to the apostles and the elders, *with the whole church*" as a consensus seeking concept. Meaning that we tried to come to a decision that is "good to everyone." At first blush, it sounds *too idealistic*, that how could everyone agree! Yes, sort of!

Also, the emphasis in Acts does seem to be on the apostles and the elders, who have to take the initial responsibility to do the part of "seems good." Meaning that they had to work together, and today's church needs to learn to pray together, to seek God's will, just like in the very beginning of the church. Afterwards, when the leaders have *consensus*, they then present it to the whole church, so that the decision is "*with* the whole church." In the text, the affirmation of the decision by the people of the church, must mean they were brought into the discussion, and must have had an opportunity to discuss, and finally *concur* with the decision.

You might say that this is impossible! But we really serve a God of the impossible, and it works, and will work. What it does make sure is that, decisions are not "rammed through," by a majority of 51, 60, nor 75%. You know that in US elections, a majority decision definitely does *not* create a sense of unity. More likely, two different "opposing camps" will emerge, and the "losing camp," surprise, is not happy! Or more likely angry or bitter. Which will sow the seeds of discontent for the future.

Whereas, where we are seeking to find out what "seems good" together, then surprisingly, we are more gentle with each other, and try not to "*beat* the other group into submission" .... Truly, we become more sensible, and more sensitive! And we try to work together, to come to a common agreement.

*每一间教会*也应该有独特性所带来的喜乐。这看起来合情理：圣灵运行并给我们独特的*教会整体的恩赐*，而每个教会又可以跟另一个教会很不一样，让我们可以真正地庆贺教会中奇妙的多样性。唯独有活泼的圣灵激励我们个人和整体，这才能实现！

3. 合一

你认为早期教会是用 51% 赞成或反对的表决方式来做决定的吗？还是 60%？75%？你怎么想呢？经文告诉我们，他们做重大决定时是要*全体同意*的。*使徒行传十五章 22 节："那时，使徒、长老并全教会都认为好……"*（新译本）

在我们教会成立的几十年里，我们采取了"*使徒、长老并全教会都认为好*"这个概念作为寻求合一的准则。这意味着我们尽力做出"每一个人都认为好"的决定。乍看之下，这听起来*太理想化*了，大家怎么都会同意？是的，几乎都是这样！

此外，使徒行传强调的重点似乎是在使徒和长老，他们要首先承担责任去做"都认为好"的那部分。也就意味着他们要一起同心同工，今天的教会需要学习一起祷告，寻求上帝的旨意，就像教会起初那样。之后，领导者达成*共识*后，就把它呈给整个教会，所以决定是"*全教会*"一起做的。在经文中，教会的弟兄姐妹肯定了那个决定，必定是意味着他们提了出来讨论，也必定有讨论的机会，最后*同意*了这个决定。

你可能会说这是不可能的！但我们就是服事不可能的上帝，而在我们的经历中，这是有效的，并且会起作用。它确保决定不是通过如 51%、60% 或 75% 等比数强行通过。你也知道在美国的选举

Please re-read the consensus verse above, more carefully again.

In another verse, the same pattern appears. *Acts 15:23-25: "...and sent them with this letter: 'The apostles and the elders, your brothers, To the brothers among the Gentiles in Antioch, Syria, and Cilicia: Greetings. It has come to our attention that some went out from us without our authorization and unsettled your minds by what they said. It seemed good to us, having become of one mind, to select men to send to you with our beloved Barnabas and Paul.'"* (New American Standard 1977)

In this verse, they decided by consensus to send Paul and Barnabas on a mission, to resolve an issue and misunderstanding. Note that "it seemed good" and "having become of one mind," clearly speak of consensus. It is good that the apostles and elders were of "one mind," something much more meaningful than "we voted, the majority outvoted the minority, the minority lost, and has to obey the majority."

同心决定——"领袖和全教会都认为好，同心"差派犹大和西拉，或巴拿巴和保罗，分别展开他们的宣道旅程。图片取自谷歌安全搜索。

Deciding by consensus, which "seemed good to the leadership with the whole church, having one mind," to send Judas and Silas, or Barnabas and Paul, on their respective missions. Google safe search, all uses. https://commons.wikimedia.org/wiki/File:Duccio_di_Buoninsegna_018.jpg

中，多数人做的决定肯定不能产生团结的感觉。更可能的是会出现两个不同意见的阵营，输掉的阵营毫无疑问会不高兴！甚至会生气或痛苦。这会为将来播下不满的种子。

然而，当我们一起致力找到"都认为好"的决定的时候，令人惊讶的是，我们对彼此都更加温柔，并尝试不去"*胁迫其他人服从*"……我们真的变得更加通情达理，更加体贴！我们会试着合作，达成共识。请再阅读上面提到合一的经文，更仔细地再读一遍。

在另一节经文中，同样的模式出现了。*使徒行传十五章23至25 节*："*于是写信交付他们，内中说：使徒和作长老的弟兄们问安提阿、叙利亚、基利家外邦众弟兄的安。我们听说，有几个人从我们这里出去，用言语搅扰你们，惑乱你们的心。其实我们并没有吩咐他们。所以，我们同心定意，拣选几个人，差他们同我们所亲爱的巴拿巴和保罗往你们那里去。*"

在这节经文中，他们一致同意决定派保罗和巴拿巴去跑一趟，解决一个问题和误解。注意"同心定意"显然是指意见一致。使徒和长老能够"同心"是很好的，比"我们投票了，多数胜过少数，少数输了，所以要服从多数"更有意义。

因此，在我们教会，属灵领袖的*意见一致*，从起初就成为我们做决定的方法。在我们的传统中，我们是以实际角度来界定意见一致——做决定时"*没有人反对*"，意思是一个人可能有一些保留，但如果他／她觉得不能确定他的*保留*是从上帝而来，那么他就"弃权"。但如果他／她经祷告后"真的反对"，这意见是受到尊重的，我们在这件事情上就"没有一致意见"。在这种情况下，我们需要继续讨论这件事，更多的祷告，*延缓*决定，以便有更多时间祷告。

在我们的历史中，我们在规模尚小时就开始了这个过程，所以

Thus, in our church, *consensus* among the spiritual leadership, from the beginning, became our approach for decision making. In our tradition of consensus, we defined it in practical terms, as decisions where there are "*no objections*," meaning one person might have some reservation but if he/she feels he cannot affirm his *reservation* as a God given one, then he "passes," or "abstains." If, however he/she has a "genuine objection" derived after prayers, it is respected, we have "no consensus." In this case, we need to discuss the issues further, pray more, and *delay* any decision for another prayer time.

In our history, we began this process when we were smaller in size, so as we grew, we generally decentralized decisions to *smaller* decision-making groups so that consensus was easier to achieve. Essentially, each smaller decision-making group had to at least have the main components of a church (*a mini-church*), in effect, an elder/minister, a deacon, (both representing larger church interests and broader wisdom), a key member of the specific interest group for the decision (representing specific expertise on the subject), and other representatives of those potentially impacted by the potential decision, for a total of something like 7 people, in order to have reasonable representation and responsibility. Thus, the concept of consensus remains, but it is a *delegated* responsibility, for efficiency.

Big decisions (defined by financial cut-points) still went from the small group, after the *first level* decision, to the entire deacons group and/ or the elder ministers group, for a further consensus and affirmation decision. The first small group basically worked out the major issues, and so the second group could build readily on that foundation, for an easier decision. Biggest issues (another financial cut-point) had to go before final decision in the "all workers group," officially representing the "entire church." For issues that were not necessarily "biggest," but the entire church should know more about, we often used an "affirmation" option for the church, more as a way of *informing* everyone for better communication, in the regular monthly combined prayer meeting.

The definition of the "all workers group," or essentially the "entire

当我们人数增长的时候，我们将决策的工作分散给*较小*的决策组，以便更容易达成共识。实际上，每个决策小组都必须有教会的组成部分（像一个*小教会*），即一位长老或牧师，一位执事（二人都代表教会整体益处和更广的智慧），与决策相关的特定组别的主要成员（代表那个题目的专家），以及可能被决定影响的其他代表。总共有 7 人左右，以便有合理的代表和负责任的人。因此，共识的概念仍然存在，但那是一项*代表性*的责任，以提高效率。

在*第一层*作出决策之后，重大的决策（由财务分割点来界定）仍然从小组提交到整个执事组和／或长老传道人组那里，以达成进一步的共识和确认的决定。第一个小组基本上解决了主要问题，因此第二组可以在此基础上稳步构建，以便更容易做出决策。最大的议题（另一个财务分割点）必须在下最终决定之前提交给"全体同工组"——"全体教会"的正式代表。对于不一定是"最大"、但整个教会应该了解更多的议题，我们通常使用"确认"这个选项，在每月定期举行的联合祷告会上*通知*各人，以保持良好的沟通。

我们教会对"全体同工组"或"全体教会"的定义相对独特。我们欢迎所有成员参加这个全体同工组的会议，参与做出任何最后的"最大决定"。但是，我们要求每个希望参加会议的人都参加*教会联合祷告*会。这个祷告会是在全体同工组的会议开始之前举行，即使因为祷告会而要把同工会推迟到晚上 8 点 30 分，也要按原定计画进行。我们就是这样坚持没有祷告（无论是公开或还是私下的），就不作决定。

因此，对于每个决定，不管大小，我们都认真地以谦卑和真诚的态度寻求上帝的指引和旨意，并相信上帝的恩典足够我们使用。上帝的教会应该比世俗社会做得*更好*，我们也应努力做到。基本上，

church group" was relatively unique. All members were welcome to come to this all workers group meeting for any final "biggest decision." But, the requirement was that everyone who wished to attend the meeting needed to attend the combined *all church prayer* meeting, held just prior to the actual "all workers" meeting hour, even if that is then pushed by the prayer meeting to 8:30 at night. That way we insisted there was no decision making without prayer, public and private.

Thus, in every decision, no matter small or big, we seriously try to seek God's direction and will, in humility and sincerity, and trust that God's grace will be sufficient for the day. God's church should work *better* than the secular world, and we must try to make it so. Basically, we must especially be willing to lay aside our personal preferences, plans, and desires for our own comfort and convenience, to submit to the Holy Spirit's leading together, in consensus as one church.

我们尤其要愿意放弃我们个人的偏好、计画，以及追求个人舒适和方便的想法，而要顺服圣灵的带领，成为合一的教会。

翻译：Grace Liu

15. Gentle Words

There is a very famous Proverb (15:1), "a soft answer turns away wrath", applicable to many communication situations. Surprisingly, many leaders do not learn this lesson early enough in their leadership careers. When they give quick, sharp answers to others, they instantly run into problems they have thoughtlessly created for themselves. By nature, my instinctive responses in my younger days tended also to be quick and sharp, so I too had to learn this practical wisdom, step by step.

During my academic leadership of a pediatric division at the hospital, I quickly learned this, and I then nudged my senior staff to also stop issuing commands or command-like memos, since these often provoked unnecessary tension. This was especially true since we were managing a group of very energetic and "feisty" neonatologists. Neonatologists are doctors for sick newborn infants. We often act like "aggressive surgeons" since, like surgeons, we also often deal with emergencies and must respond quickly and precisely to save a very small baby's life. This kind of temperament easily translates into difficulties at work, because we act quickly and respond sharply, and often might be hypersensitive to provocations, especially words that seem not so soft, especially from an "official" figure! However, I have often learned that it's definitely not just neonatologists; many people can have similar "prickliness".

Rather unconsciously, I fell into a rather unusual habit of writing my communications to my division as "Reggiegrams," a term given affectionately by my staff. Reggiegrams are my personal invention, I suppose, where I did

15. 柔和的言语

有一句耳熟能详的箴言："回答柔和,使怒消退"(箴言十五1),可应用在各种场合的沟通上。令人惊讶的是,不少身居领导位置的人未能早早就学到这功课。他们惯于迅速尖锐地应答,于是就粗心大意地给自己制造了麻烦。我年轻的时候也是这样按照本能作出反应,结果我慢慢地学到了这智慧。

在医院儿科部负责学术领导的时候,我很快就学到这功课,也提醒我的高级职员不要发号施令或写带命令性质的备忘录,因为这些做法往往会引起一些不必要的矛盾。当时我们管理的是一群精力旺盛、桀骜不驯的新生儿科专家,因此更需要留意。新生儿科医生是负责给新生儿看病。我们做事的方式往往像是"攻势凌厉的外科医生",因为我们就像外科医生一样,经常要应付急诊,必须迅速而准确地作出反应,以抢救初生婴儿垂危的生命。这种环境常常使得我们似乎很难合作,因为我们必须迅速地直奔主题,容易把领导层某些硬梆梆的用词视为挑衅,因而会有过激反应。后来我发现这种"敏感性"不只局限于新生儿科医生,其实许多人都有。

我无意中养成了一个不寻常的习惯,就是亲笔写下给我整个部门的通知或备忘录,我的同事更把它们昵称为"曾式语记,Reggiegrams"。这是我个人的发明,我不是通过打字发出官僚式的"部门通知",也不会让我的秘书代我发出(这样做会更糟),而

not type out formal bureaucratic-like "memos" and I certainly did not allow my secretary to send them on my behalf, which would have been even worse. I wrote out my quasi-memos by hand, often without commas and periods, short and brief, line-by-line "thoughts", more like "poetry", as someone once graciously said to me. There was no formal clean, typed-up official look. We simply made Xerox copies of them for circulation -- this was before the era of emails, if you can imagine that.

My Reggiegrams were informal and casual, as if we were engaging in some sort of chat. They certainly were far from the look of edicts or commands, even though they might have ultimately had a similar intention. But they gave the understanding that there was always room for negotiation or dialogue, if necessary, which is nearly always true anyway, even for edicts. The only downside was that sometimes the messages could seem a bit "poetically" cryptic. It was kind of more like a forerunner of today's young people's "messaging" style! You see, dialogue is always more chatty and "informal", since there is an implication of humility, that there is always room to improve. An impression of thoughts not totally developed, "t"s not exactly all crossed, and "i"s not all dotted, more likely fits the concept and implications of the "soft answer".

While somewhat informal, clearly it was my signal and message of respect to the recipients not to issue a "command from above". To even further indicate goodwill, I often included a touch of humor, which definitely reduced tension. Emojis of smiley faces had not yet been invented back then, but the intention was similar. Indeed, we were, in reality, all colleagues and partners in service together, no one being the King! The only slight problem, which could even be comical, was that a colleague might come up to the secretary to try to decipher my "doctor's handwriting", or to ask whether there was another meaning to my relatively cryptic note! Which was no problem, since the next Reggiegram gave me a chance to clarify the message, again implying openness to dialogue.

Let's think this through. Why are we sending out the communication in

是亲笔写下我的"想法",常常没有标点符号,一行行短小简练,有人曾很客气地说更像是写诗。没有一般打字的官方格式,那会儿还没有电子邮件,我们只是复印一下我的手写稿就分发给大家。

我的"曾式语记"感觉随意,如同在聊天,完全没有官样通告的那种正儿八经,虽然要传达的讯息是一样,但给人感觉有讨论协商的余地,而情况也几乎总是这样,即便是法令也不例外。唯一不足之处就是有时我要传达的讯息看起来有点"诗意",不那么直接。犹如现在年轻人传的"简讯",我的曾式语记算是先例!对话式的沟通总是随意而不那么正式,隐含着谦卑,让人觉得不是一言堂,可以有余地改进。这样的简讯看起来并不一定是完全成熟、已经有定论,而更像是切合"回答柔和"的概念和含意。

虽然并不像官方通告,但这些讯息显然是出于我对收信者的尊重,用以代替"上级通知"。有时我会融合一点幽默,更显善意,一点小幽默常常就能或多或少化解一些紧张气氛。当年还没有发明电子笑脸,但用意差不多。我们都是同事,有共同使命的合作伙伴,没有高高在上的王!只有一个小问题,甚至是有点滑稽的,就是有时同事会跑来问我的秘书,我用"医生体"所写的某句话到底是什么意思,或者问我的半谜语式写法是不是隐含了另一层意思!这都不是问题,因为我可以在下一期曾式语记中解释清楚,这样就有了开放的对话互动。

我们来想一想,我们一开始是为了什么发这些讯息?一般是为了产生我们认为必要的一些行为上的改变。通常我们并不想像"立法"那样正儿八经地公布新条规,那样常常会引起反感甚至愤怒!柔和的回答会让人心平气和地思考所面对的问题,没有愤怒,没有负面情绪,因此可以更理性地消化所收到的讯息。像曾式语记这样

the first place? The usual reason for sending out some sort of a memo, or even an edict, is to achieve some change in behavior which we think is needed. We do not really mean to issue a command as if we were "the Law". It's certainly not meant to deliberately create a negative reaction or anger! A soft answer allows people to think through the issue in a peaceful way, without anger or other negative emotions, so that they can more logically process the communication. "Non-memo communications" (including Reggiegrams) invite true dialogue and not reactive anger. Again, the value of a "soft answer".

My only caveat is that in a traditional authoritarian environment, this might be confusing to some people who may be more used to "edicts", so the response might be awkward. And this style might take some getting used to, since this style could be rather new. I think I offended someone that way, in an Asian setting when I was the Executive Director of the medical mission I co-founded. This person, a surgeon, interpreted my informality as being disrespectful of the position I was in. In a sense he was correct, that I really had less regard for official hierarchies! There is little need for that in most circumstances anyway, if we do our job well.

In any committee meeting that I chaired or was the general secretary (the best job in the committee, by far), I would always try to summarize the discussion of the committee in a positive, thoughtful and soft manner for the minutes that were to be sent around to attendees and other persons who needed to know. Further, I would always clearly label any major decision initially as "DRAFT". This key word "DRAFT" was a practically magical way of being a softer answer. It meant that the conclusions in the minutes were not ironclad, like a command, but that the plan was being formed and crafted with lots of input, and that every committee member still had the opportunity of helping in its final formulation. Or to correct any misinterpretation of comments made during the heat of discussion.

No one should feel insulted, and everyone's input was appreciated. Afterwards, many drafts later, then the document could be made "final". Except even then I avoided the word "final". I often felt instinctively that there

的"非备忘录式的沟通",能促进真正的对话而不是引起愤怒。这再次突显了"回答柔和"的重要性。

要切记的是,在着重威权的非西方文化环境当中,这对有些人可能有点不好理解,因为他们习惯于听"指令",所以这样的答复可能会让他们觉得有点模棱两可。这种风格对他们来说是新事物,需要时间来适应。我想我就犯过这样的错误。当时在亚洲,我是一项我有分发起的医疗事工的执行主任,对方是一个外科医生,他把我这种比较随性的沟通方式理解成为我对自己的职位不尊重。从某个角度来讲,他是对的,因为我不是那么在乎正式的层级制度!只要我们大家都把自己的事情干好,在大多数情况下是上级或下级都不重要。

每次我主持一个委员会会议或是担任大会秘书长(这是我最喜欢做的职位),我都会经过仔细斟酌,用正面积极、柔和的措辞,把委员会讨论的内容总结一下,发给与会者和其他需要通知的人。我总会把任何委员会的决定,一开始就标明是"草案"。"草案"这个词,其实就是一个柔和的答案。它意味着会议记录里的这些决定不是铁板钉钉的不能改变,不是一道指令,而是说我们经过多方考虑后初步达成了一个方案,每一个成员还有机会可以影响最后的决议。草案也可以用来纠正在热烈讨论过程中有可能被误解的一些意见。

这样,没有人会感到不被尊重。每一个人都可以各抒己见。经过很多轮这样的草案,"最终"方案就形成了,但是一般我都避免使用"最终"这个词。我本能地认为实际上真的没有最终方案这么一说,我一般只是简单地用一个日期来标注这份档,实际上还是像一个草案一样。无论理论上还是实际上,总是有可以改进的余地!并且"最终"这个词,让人觉得不那么柔和。

were really no final, final documents, so I often just left it simply as a date-identified document, still in fact like a draft, which in theory and in practice could always be improved at a later time! The word "final" really sounds "not soft".

Similarly, in a church setting, leaders often innocently give edicts or command-like memos, which they think are effective ways to communicate with church members, but which could instantly provoke reactions difficult to predict or manage. In perspective, it's good to remember that kings and historical patriarchs loved to give edicts, but those were in totally different eras and cultures, so maybe those are not our best role models.

Even if a committee of well-intentioned people gets together to make some sort of a decision, the resulting decision and announcement memo can often really sound like some sort of a harsh command or edict. This is especially so if the decision is primarily directed towards a small group of people, or even one person, in which case the memo could even, in the worst case, read like a "prosecution document from a tribunal". Like the term "ganging up on someone". All these are, of course, very far from "a soft answer turns away wrath", and I believe these should be avoided. So, crafting the decision statement in as soft a manner as possible, not as an edict, but more as a tentative decision, expressed in a sincerely humble, sort of even a Reggiegram style, will work wonders.

I kind of think that, in contrast to biblical commands, such as the Ten Commandments or the direct commands of Jesus, there are very few immutable commands or edicts from man that really last or that are really that good. Even from the Pope! Even if a major decision is made today, circumstances could significantly change next year, and the decision may have to be changed! Even if it is the Supreme Court. It is too easy for us to naively assume that our decisions are the best decisions ever made. Really?

Actually, part of the practical secret of the soft answer is to try not to hurry decisions and conclusions along too much, since that instantly makes them less soft! Let the issue percolate, give time for ideas to soak in, and give

15. 柔和的言语
15. Gentle Words

同样在教会里，领导者一般都会无意中就给了方案或者指令式的备忘录。他们认为这样可以非常有效地和教会会友沟通。但有时候这样会马上激起某些难以预测或难以掌控的反应。回过头来看。在历史上任何时期，国王或者大人物都喜欢下诏，发号司令。但他们都是身处截然不同的时代和文化，不见得是我们最好的榜样。

Decision Making Principles at CCC

(Draft 11.19.07)

Key Verses

1) Discussions of <u>key groups</u> made by consensus

Acts: ("we agreed")

- *Act 15:12* - All the people kept silent, and they were <u>listening</u> to Barnabas and Paul as they were relating what signs and wonders God had done through them among the Gentiles.
- *22* - Then it <u>seemed good to the apostles and the elders, with the whole church,</u> to choose men from among them to send to Antioch with Paul and Barnabas--Judas called Barsabbas, and Silas, leading men among the brethren,
- *25* - it seemed good to us, having become of one mind, to select men to

草稿之后是另一个草稿，隐含着"柔和的回答"和"谦卑"。也就是说，我们在这些问题上需要一步一步地解决，而不是就给一个命令。图中的例子说明在教会里是如何做决定的：用圣经里的原则来建构草案。

Drafts and drafts are an implicit expression of "soft answer" and "humility" that we need to work on issues step by step; they are not edicts. An example of a developing decision at church, framing a draft with bible verse concepts.

即使是一群出于善意的人在一起做出一个决定，一般来说，他们的决定以及后来公布的方式，也可能听起来就好像是在发号施令，尤其是如果这个决定是针对一小部分人或是针对某一个人。有时候甚至糟糕至极，如同法庭宣判，或群起攻之。这些当然是跟"回答柔和，使怒消退"相去甚远，我认为这种情况应该避免。所以，在表述一个决定的时候措词应该尽量柔和，不是好像写一道圣旨，而更像是表述一个暂时的决定，用真诚、谦卑的方式表达，甚至是像"曾式语记"的风格，这样往往会产生奇妙的效果。

有时候我想，与圣经里的十诫以及耶稣的直接命令截然不同的是：从人的角度来讲，几乎没有什么不可更改的命令或决议能够

法庭还是会颁布法令的，尤其是最高法院。但即使是
最高法院的决议，后来也会更改。他们不是上帝。
Courts of law still issue edicts...especially the Supreme
Court. But even then, there are later changes. They are not
God. From https://georgewbush-whitehouse.archives.gov/
news/releases/2005/10/images/20051003_d-0143-515h.
html

time for others to have input and to understand the usually complex factors involved; all of these processes are ingredients of a soft answer. You will then be amazed how much better decisions are accepted, and therefore best executed.

The first draft provides a framework, a starting point, a way of focusing ideas, but in the subsequent drafts, the input, molding and acceptance of good ideas can create a document with softness and not harshness. Give each word in the drafts careful thought, and if possible, even add a deliberate "soft touch", so even if the final message is a relatively "tough" one, acceptance is built into it. Expressed with love, especially God's love.

Church decisions obviously should all be made in accordance with bible references and principles, and the drafts should include these references. However, we still might misinterpret bible references, so our communications are always tentative, even if laced with bible principles. All the wonderful bible verses are actually there to remind us that there really is a true enduring reference manual of true commands and edicts. But, get this, in which the "greatest is love" is the greatest edict that overwhelms all other commands. And love is caring, especially in communicating to a church that God loves immensely.

Finally, when church committees, ministers, or elders communicate to others in a "spirit of humility", which really is the key point, the underlying implication of "a soft answer", people sense immediately that the

15. 柔和的言语
15. Gentle Words

长久有效或是那么完美无瑕。哪怕天主教教皇颁布的，亦是如此！今天做了一个特别重要的决定，但是情况或许在下一年就变了，这个决定就得更改！甚至是最高法院的决议也一样。有时候我们很容易会异想天开，很幼稚地认为我们的决定是史上最好的。真是这样吗？

实际上，回答柔和的一个实用的秘诀，就是不要匆匆忙忙下决定或者得出结论，因为这样马上就令它们变得柔和！让这些事情慢慢地沉淀消化，让这些想法慢慢地进入每个人的思维，让大家有时间来给予回馈，来理解复杂的相关因素。这些过程就是柔和答案的原材料。你会很惊讶，这种方式竟然使人更容易接受、因此更好地执行决定。

第一份草案提供了一个框架，作为讨论的一个基点，用以征集大家的意见。然后随着大家的回馈、讨论，一些好主意渐渐成形，这样就能用柔和而不是严苛的措词写成一个档案。经过字斟句酌，如果可能的话，特意加一点柔和的言语，即使最后这个方案比较"强硬"，接受起来也会容易一些。用爱来表达，尤其是上帝的爱。

教会的决定显然要按照圣经的真理和原则，草案当中也应该注明这些参照。但是我们还是有可能会误解所引用的圣经原则，所以，哪怕我们参照了很多圣经的原则，我们的草案都总是属于初步的。圣经里所有奇妙的经文其实都是要提醒我们，的确有一个真正永存的参考指南，其中有真正的命令。但是要知道，"最大的是爱"这一条就是最大的命令，它超越了其他一切指令。而爱就是关心，尤其是在与教会的会众沟通的时候更要着重爱，因为上帝非常爱教会。

最后，教会的一些委员会、传道人或者长执要以"谦卑的灵"来与会众沟通。这一点至关重要，也是"回答柔和"蕴含的意义。

communication is not meant to demonstrate superiority or power but, rather, a sincere desire to do our best through God's wisdom. Together. A soft answer turns away wrath.

这才是一个永不改变的真正命令。

Now this is truly an edict which never changes. From https://www.flickr.com/groups/the_phillip_medhurst_collection_of_bible_prints/pool/phillip_medhurst_bible_pictures

15. 柔和的言语
15. Gentle Words

这样的话，会众就马上感受到这样的沟通并不是发号施令，而是真诚地想以属天的智慧合力做到最好。回答柔和，就能使怒消退。

翻译：Dixia

16. Money Matters

Money issues in church can be a hassle, but guess what the keys to understanding it are? Surprise! The keys are principles straight from within the pages of the greatest book! These money-related principles, if taught early in life to children and youth, are a great foundation for life. And the early church, 2,000 years ago, composed mostly of young adults (Jesus was only 30 years old), is still a *great model* for church management and money issues, even for today! It was clearly a great guide to us when we started our Cincinnati church in 1970.

Startlingly, when we read about money issues in the early church, right away we are reminded that the one who betrayed Jesus was actually the *treasurer* of Jesus' own church, the first church in the world. One of the twelve original disciples *personally* selected by Jesus in the very beginning of His ministry. The treasurer, a key member of any team, was the one who did the worst evil, by betraying his Master! Corruption (stealing from the money bag) and betrayal (by instigating the arrest and "sale" of Jesus), right in the bosom of Jesus! Lesson 1: *We are indeed all sinners*, even those chosen by God, even those chosen to handle His money, and may the mercy of God cover us.

In another unusual stroke, Jesus also brought in a tax collector, Matthew, a Jewish man experienced in handling money, to be another member of His core team. Today, "Jewish finance professionals" are reputedly adept at managing finances, but Jewish tax collectors of the time were generally not respected. So, Matthew's selection might have seemed initially more like a *bad* idea, maybe even to the other disciples, but Jesus was (and is) in the

16. 钱很重要

钱的问题在教会里可能是一个麻烦，但是猜猜什么是理解它的关键？让你吓一跳！关键直接来自那本最伟大的书里面的原则！那些与钱有关的原则，如果在人们儿时和青年时就教给他们，将会是他们生命中的伟大基石。在 2,000 年前，主要由年轻人（耶稣也才 30 岁）组成的早期教会，仍然是今日教会管理和金钱问题的*楷模*！它显然也是我们辛城教会在 1970 年建立时的伟大指南。

令人惊讶的是，当我们读到早期教会的金钱问题时，我们马上就会想到那个出卖耶稣的人实际上是耶稣自己的教会、也就是世界上第一间教会里的*财务员*。他是耶稣在开始宣道时*亲自*拣选的十二门徒之一。无论在任何组织里，财务员都是一个关键成员，但他竟是那个出卖他的主的罪大恶极之人！腐败（他从钱袋里偷了钱）和背叛（他策画如何抓捕

我们都是罪人：我们要提醒自己，犹大是一个核心成员、第一间教会的财务员，也是第一个信徒群体中负责管理钱袋的人，但是他却背叛了耶稣。图片取自谷歌安全搜索。

We are all sinners: we remind ourselves of a core team member, the first church treasurer, Judas, the handler of the money bag for the first Fellowship of believers, but who betrayed Jesus. From Google safe search, all uses. https://farm2.staticflickr.com/1701/25009210332_cd20c4a41e_n.jpg

business of changing sinners. He obviously knew that tax collectors, even like the evil Zaccheus, could be rehabilitated and *transformed* into great disciples. By the Lord. Lesson 2: We are sinners saved by grace, changed by His grace so that we can do great things.

In the handling of money, therefore, we must be forewarned at many levels. Our money skills are often learned from the secular world, so we need to be careful what we might *unconsciously* bring into church. For example, if "love of money is the root of all evil" (I Timothy 6:10), and yet the world's operative driving force *is often the love of money*, what we learn from the world about money must be very suspect. I suggest that we actually learn to *flip the logic*. In other words, if "love of money is the root of all evil", we as a church could deliberately live as a church that does *not love* money, to wither the root of evil! And we should faithfully teach this in both church and family, especially to the next generation. Now that would be refreshing! Lesson 3: The root of evil withers when the church lives a life that doesn't love money.

Emphases and priorities

How any church views money is seen in *how it spends* its money. Commonly, we spend a lot more on ourselves, compared with spending for others. "Where our money is, that's where our hearts are," (Matthew 6:21), was written down by *Matthew, the Jewish finance man*, who had originally learned his money skills from the secular world. But he had watched and listened as Jesus *constantly* preached about caring for the poor and wretched, the prisoner and the neglected, the sick and the disabled. Obviously, Jesus was *very* concerned about them, and Matthew took that to heart and relayed that to us all. One good question to ask ourselves, therefore, would be, "Are we similarly concerned?" One quick look at the actual expenses incurred by our church will quickly reveal the *value and concern we place* on each work and ministry.

In income categories, Asian Americans as a group are in the top 1% of the

和"卖"耶稣),就在耶稣的胸前!第一课:*我们的确全都是罪人*,甚至那些被上帝所选的人,甚至那些被选来掌管祂的钱财的人。愿上帝的怜悯复庇我们。

另外一个非同寻常的举动是,耶稣也把税吏马太,一个有管理钱财经验的犹太人,带进祂的核心团队。今天,"犹太金融专家"在金融管理上应该很有才能,可是犹太人税吏在那时一般不受尊重。所以,选择马太起初看来更像是一个*坏*主意,也许连其他门徒也有同感。可是,耶稣那时(和现在)是做改变罪人的生意。祂显然知道税吏,甚至像恶魔税吏撒该,也能被治愈并*改造*成伟大的门徒。被上帝改造。第二课:我们是被恩典拯救的罪人,被祂的恩典改变,能去做伟大的工作。

因此,在管理钱财时,我们必须在很多层面预先收到警告。通常我们管理金钱的技巧是从世俗世界学来的,所以我们需要小心,看看我们有可能*不经意地*把什么带进教会。举个例子,如果"贪财是万恶之根"(提摩太前书六10),而推动世界运作的又*往往是贪财*,那么,我们从世界所学的关于金钱的知识就一定值得怀疑。我建议我们其实要学习*颠倒这个逻辑*。换言之,如果"贪财是万恶之根",那么,我们教会的生活就可以特意地*不爱钱财*,让万恶之根枯萎!我们还应该忠心地在教会和家庭,特别对下一代教导这功课。这将会焕然一新!第三课:当教会过一种不爱钱财的生活,万恶之根就会枯萎。

强调和优先

教会看待金钱的方式会在*它怎样使用*钱财上看出来。通常,我

world, clearly fitting the description of the rich in the bible. And, we clearly *worry* more about money than Jesus did. Matthew sharply recorded Jesus in 6:26 as saying, "Even birds of the air do not have to worry about themselves, for the heavenly Father looks after them," reminding us of our usually *un*biblical attitudes towards money. This verse likely applies especially to the rich, who clearly have *more* accounts to worry about! And to their next generation, who have grown up in luxury without even realizing it. Surely, in a counter-cultural way, one of the great *financial reasons* for *missions* is that the church and each one of us, younger or older, quickly realize that we should stop worrying about our own finances, and should seriously pray about what we should really do, biblically, with our vast resources. For others.

Concern for *others* opens up the window of true/realistic/practical/ immediate/authentic/touching compassion for all. Few individuals, or even churches, have developed the good habit of *regular giving* to those who are disadvantaged. Nor have they carefully taught their children and youth. The *inspiration* derived from the *act of regular giving*, as opposed to "money hoarding", especially in the lives of rich Asians, is usually far better than long pulpit sermons! Open our own windows, our children's windows, and the church's windows, and heaven promises to open its windows of blessings on us! (See Malachi 3:10.) Personally, my wife and I learned that lesson early in childhood, and undoubtedly it has been a wonderful lifelong blessing for us. It works the same great way for a church, and each new generation needs to learn that, especially from early life.

The church finance committee

The church finance committee functions illustrate many church money issues, and the principles guiding the committee apply in general to all use of church money. Remember first, whenever we set up any church committee, it needs a *spiritual* focus, not just a functional one. The real focus and reason is Jesus, so those handling finances should learn to encourage and *pray* for

们花在我们自己身上的钱比花在别人身上的更多。"因为你的财宝在哪里，你的心也在那里"（马太福音六 21）——这是*犹太人财务师马太*所写的，他最初是从世俗世界里学到管理钱财的技能。但是，在耶稣*不断*宣讲要照顾穷人和不幸的人、囚犯和被忽略的人、生病的人和残疾人时，他亦在旁观看和聆听。显然，耶稣*非常*关心他们，马太也用心谨记，然后传达给我们所有人。有一个很好的问题我们可以问自己："我们亦同样关心吗？"只要看一下我们教会的实际开支，很快就展示出*我们有多着重和关心*各项工作和事工。

在收入方面，亚裔美国人这个群体是世界上顶尖的 1%，清楚地符合圣经所指的富人。而且，我们也显然比耶稣更*担心*钱财。马太尖锐地记载了耶稣的话："你们看那天上的飞鸟，也不种，也不收，也不积蓄在仓里，你们的天父尚且养活它"（马太福音六26），提醒我们对待金钱的态度往往是*不符合*圣经的。这节经文可能对富人尤其合用，他们显然有*更多户口*需要担心！对他们那些在奢侈的环境里成长也不自觉的下一代，这节经文就更有意义。确实，为*宣道提供资金*的其中一个好理由，就是让教会和我们各人，不分老幼，都很快就意识到我们不应再为自己的财务忧虑，而要认真祷告，找出我们应该用我们庞大的资源做些什么合乎圣经的事情、为他人而做的事情。这是一种抗衡文化的方式。

关心*他人*打开了一扇窗，让我们真正／务实／实际／立刻／真诚／感人地怜悯所有人。很少有人，甚或是教会，已经养成了*定期捐献*给弱势群体的好习惯。他们也没有细心地教导他们的孩子和青少年。定期捐献跟"囤积金钱"是刚好相反的行动；特别是对富有的亚洲人来说，源自*定期捐献这行动*的*激励*，通常远远比在讲坛上讲长篇的道要好得多！打开我们的窗、我们孩子的窗和教会的窗

each other, for wisdom, and for Jesus' *love* to be pre-eminent in all local and mission money needs.

As with most church committees, the finance committee helps the church and its leaders, but *not* as *a governing body*. It should not set financial policy; that is an elders and/ or deacons function. Having an elder or deacon on the committee provides experience and biblical wisdom, to help guide its *spiritual* functions. As an elder, I often led money-related devotionals or told relevant missionary stories to set a good frame for committee discussions. And I reminded the group to pray *during* complex discussions, to seek God's will, and not just have ritualistic blessing prayers at the beginning and end.

呼召财务员马太加入团队。虽然马太参与了一份被人仇恨的、只着重金钱的工作，但他却被改变了，转而事奉上帝，用他的技能写下详尽而著名的福音书。上帝也能改变我们。图片取自谷歌安全搜索。

Calling of Matthew, the finance man, to join the team. Even though Matthew had been involved in a hated money-driven profession, he was changed to serve God with his technical skills to write his detailed and famous gospel. God can change us also. From Google safe search, all uses. https://farm9.staticflickr.com/8256/29338608455_d28532e727_b.jpg

Note that finance team members should *not* be brought on board just because they are experienced accountants or secular finance people. The true character of servants is best found through their actual work in ministries. *Luke 16:10 "He who is faithful in a very little thing is faithful also in much; and he who is unrighteous in a very little thing is unrighteous also in much."* Finance members definitely need to have been "tested." There was a McDonald's story going around in Asia that one of the first steps for promotion in the Company was to pass the test of cleaning its restaurant toilets well. This makes sense, when you think about how important cleanliness is in this industry. And in church finances.

Finance committee members should also personally support church

16. 钱很重要
16. Money Matters

吧，天上的窗户也必敞开，倾福与我们！（参看玛拉基书三10）个人而言，我和妻子在年幼时就学了这一课，它毫无疑问地成为我们一生的祝福。它对教会也发挥同样重要的功能，每一个新世代的人都需要学习，特别是要从小就学习。

教会财务委员

教会财务委员的功能阐明了教会里许多金钱的问题，指导着委员会的原则也普遍适用于教会里所有用钱的事宜。首先要记住，每当我们在教会里设立委员会，都需要一个*属灵的*焦点，而不是仅仅着眼于功能。真正的焦点和原因是耶稣，所以那些掌管财务的人应该学习去相互鼓励和*代祷*，祈求得到智慧和耶稣的*爱*，能好好处理地方和宣道上的所有金钱的需要。

跟教会中的大多数委员会一样，财务委员会对教会和它的带领者都有帮助，但它*不是作为一个管理的团体*。它不应该设立钱财使用的原则，因为那是长老和执事的工作。委员会里有长老或执事，目的是提供经验和合乎圣经的智慧，帮助它发挥*属灵上的*功能。作为长老，我经常带领委员做与金钱相关的灵修，或是讲一些相关的宣道士的故事，以便为委员会的讨论定好基调。我还提醒大家在激烈的讨论*期间*祷告，寻求上帝的旨意，而不只是在开头和结尾时做例行的祷告。

请注意，我们*不应该*只因为某些人有会计师或世俗财务的经验就吸收他们成为财务委员会成员。仆人的真品性最能够在他们教会的事奉上表现出来。*路加福音十六章10节："人在最小的事上忠心，在大事上也忠心；在最小的事上不义，在大事上也不义。"* 财务委

financial needs, since *"where your treasure is, there your heart will be also"* *Matthew again, 6:21.* Involve them in prayer meetings, so they will know the needs of less visible ministries, such as poverty or overseas missions areas, to bring prayer for these ministries into finance committee discussions, to give a *spiritual*, rather than purely technical perspective.

It's best to stay away from excessive fund raising in church, however well intentioned, because of the potential for coercion and blowback. More prayer is biblical, and leaders should simply show the financial needs, since *tithing* is still the best biblical time-tested "mechanism" for raising support. Which is clearly something that should be taught from early childhood, weekly, through the act of offerings at church. This extremely powerful and meaningful discipline has been a guiding principle all through our own lives, and is attested by many as truly valuable for all walks of life.

Pastors and money

It's important for the church to strongly support the ministers in their financial needs. It is a travesty to impoverish the ministers while the congregation has abundant resources. The best practical principle is the principle of averages. Elders prayerfully meet to set the level of ministerial support at around an estimated *average*, considering the average incomes of ministers in the state, of high school teachers, and of state residents. This is based on biblical verses like Proverbs 30:8, expressing the reasonable expectation of believers "not to be rich or poor". Important needs such as health care and retirement funds should be fully covered, just like any citizen. The next generation especially needs to learn how and why decisions are made in church, and finance decisions such as support for ministers and missionaries are good learning areas. They can apply these lessons when they become future deacons and leaders of many churches.

We learned by experience that it was best if ministers were not directly involved with church finances. The finance committee should help *protect*

16. 钱很重要
16. Money Matters

员会成员一定必须被"测试过"。在亚洲流传着一个关于麦当劳快餐店的故事：要在公司里晋升的其中一步，就是先通过清洁店里的马桶的测试。当你想想清洁对这个行业有多重要，就会发现这很正常。教会的财务也是如此。

财务委员会成员本身也应该支持教会的财务需要，因为"*你的财宝在哪里，你的心也在那里*"（马太福音六 21）。带他们参加祷告会，让他们知道不太显眼的事工的需要，比如关注穷人和海外的宣道地区，在财务委员会的讨论中为这些事工祷告，带来一个*属灵*而不单纯是技术的角度。

因为有可能出现强制和反弹的情况，所以不管初始意愿有多好，教会最好不要过度募捐。更多的祷告更符合圣经的教导，带领者也应该只表明财政的需要，因为*十一奉献*仍是合乎圣经、被时间验证过的筹集资金的最佳"方式"。这项教导显然也应该在儿童年幼时，每周透过教会的奉献行动灌输给他们。这个极为有力和有意义的操练是我们一生的指导原则，也被无数人验证过，认为它对各行各业的人都的确是真正有价值的原则。

牧师和金钱

对教会而言，慷慨支持牧者很重要。当会众有着丰富资源的时候却让牧者活在贫穷中是可笑的。最好的实用原则是平均。长老们敬虔地聚集一起，以州内的牧师、高中教师和州内居民的平均薪酬来估算一个*平均数*，用以设定给牧师的薪水。这是根据圣经经文如箴言三十章 8 节，表达出信徒"不贫穷也不富足"的合理期望。重要的需要譬如健康保险和退休金应该完全涵盖，就像任何公民都

the minister from such worries, and especially any unfair accusations from disgruntled members, such as for *apparent* financial "conflict of interest". For example, special donations can create awkward scenarios, for example, wills naming the church as recipient, but disputed by family members. Make sure ministers do not get "sucked into" these messes. An elder or finance committee person can better deal with such awkward issues.

Mission needs

Encouraging church members in *free-will offerings* for, say, short-term missions, is a sensible way to raise missions support, instead of "sales" of any kind. The young mission team learns to be involved in love, for example, by *giving out* gifts of baked goods or tribal bags, bracelets and necklaces, while church members should simply be encouraged to give, and not feel coerced. Stay away from directly selling things or trying to "make money in the church" or anything like the historic temple money changers, who encountered the angry Jesus! Remember that the Reformation, now 500 years ago, was *precipitated* by the "worst money-making project" in church history, selling indulgences to help build St. Peter's Church, possibly a noble goal, but certainly an *unbiblical practice*, amazingly directed from top church leadership.

激励现代众多信徒的一大良机，就是去支援、探访宣道士，并为他们祷告。他们前往偏远地方，在贫穷的儿童中间服事，这些儿童就像耶稣在世时村庄里的孩子一样。

One of the greatest opportunities to encourage many modern-day believers, "functional millionaires" by historical and worldwide standards, is to support, visit and pray for, missionaries in far-away places, among poverty-stricken children, just like village children of Jesus' time.

应该得到的保障。下一代特别需要学习教会里的决定是怎样和为什么做出来的，资助牧者和宣道士等财务决定是很好的学习范围。这样，当他们未来成为多个教会的执事和带领者时，就可以应用这些功课。

我们通过经验学到，牧者们最好还是不要直接参与教会的财务。财务委员会应该帮助*保护*牧者免于这样的担忧，尤其是来自于不满的会友那些不公平的指控，像是*表面上*的财务“利益冲突”。例如，特殊的奉献能制造尴尬的剧情，譬如遗嘱指定教会为受益者，可是家人却提出异议。要确保牧者不被“卷进”这些纷争中。由长老或财务委员会的成员来处理这类棘手的问题会更好。

宣道需要

鼓励教会会友为如短宣等事工*自愿地奉献*，是筹集宣道资金的一种理智的方式，而不是任何形式的“推销”。年轻的宣道团队学习用爱心参与，譬如是*送出*烘培食品，或者是民族小礼袋、手镯和项链等作为礼物；对于会友，教会则应该直接鼓励他们奉献，却不会令他们感到被迫。别直接推销物品或尝试“在教会中赚钱”，或者从事圣殿中兑换银钱者所做的那类买卖——他们遇到了愤怒的耶稣！要记住，*触发*距今 500 年的宗教改革的，是教会历史上“最糟的赚钱计画”——兜售赎罪券以建造圣彼得大教堂。这也许是一个高尚的目标，可是*做法*却绝对*不符合圣经*，而令人惊讶的是，计画竟来自当时教会的领袖。

宣道的需要经常给教会带来很大的挑战，因为我们经常要同时面教会内迫切的需要。恰当的反应是真的要更多祷告，为上帝的旨

Mission needs often pose great challenges to any church, since we always have to also cope with pressing local needs. The proper response is truly more prayer, both for God's will and His touching of church members' hearts. As a consequence, we learn a lot each time about our own attitudes of "hoarding" versus "giving". Pray that we are not the "one-Talent man" who *refused to use the Talent* the Master gave him, on the erroneous assumption that his "harsh master" wanted him to *hoard* it, instead of *using* it... no! Our loving Master definitely wants us to use the Talents (money) He gave us for His kingdom!! He even severely punished the "one-Talent man" as "evil."

Finally, in working with missionaries, beware of stressing them out with onerous bureaucratic western rules, based on the *misconception* that the IRS is demanding it. Our unique country has solid church/state *separation* principles, so unless we are stealing money, we have a lot of leeway in decisions regarding how we manage missionary finances, just like in our normal local operations. After all, the main function of churches *is the Great Commission,* exactly what missionaries are normally doing. The best approach is to love the missionaries, be generous, and help them to set up a local on-site board for accountability. Frontline workers with limited or no resources should not have to waste their time on excessive paperwork.

Now, wasn't that fun? Money issues are challenging, but when money is wisely spent, there can be hugely good impact and joy for generations to come.

意祈求，也祈求祂感动教会会众的心。结果，我们每一次都学到很多——究竟我们的态度是"囤积"还是"给予"。祈求上帝使我们不会成为那个"拿了一千银子的仆人"，他*拒绝用主人所给的银两*，错误地假设他这个"苛刻的主人"想他把银子*囤积*起来，而不是*使用*它……不！爱我们的主一定想要我们把祂所赐给我们的银子（金钱）用在祂的国度上！！祂甚至严厉地惩罚了那个"拿了一千银子的仆人"，认为他"又恶又懒"。

最后，在与这些宣道士同工的时候，别让他们担忧西方繁琐官僚的规矩，*误以为*那是美国税务局的要求。美国这个独特的国家有稳固的政教*分离*的原则，所以除非我们偷钱，否则我们有很大的自由来决定我们如何管理宣道方面的财务，就像决定教会内正常的花费一样。毕竟，教会的主要功能是实践*大使命*，那正是宣道士正常的工作。最好的方法是爱宣道士，慷慨解囊，帮助他们建立一个当地的财务行政管理委员会，以便交代。前线的同工在毫无资源或资源有限的情况下，就不应该把时间浪费在文件上。

来到这里，觉得有趣吗？金钱问题是有挑战性的，可是若能明智地使用金钱，它会起很大的作用，为未来的世代带来美好的效果和喜乐。

翻译：Dan Zhao

17. The Fun of Starting a New Ministry

As elder from the beginning of our church in Cincinnati, I have been acting minister *7 times* in its history, and every time it seemed like we were starting a new church, and I could relive the excitement and fun of that again, and again. The reason I say it is fun is that *it is fun*. Included in the 7 times were indeed the first time when we began the church in 1970, 50 years ago; the time when we began the youth program; and the time we began the English congregation; plus the times when ministers had gone on to other roles, and I had to substitute for the year or more in their absence. So, in a sense, I have been blessed with wonderful opportunities to help start many ministries "from scratch," or near scratch. Indeed, I truly believe, each time an exciting and joyful time in any enterprise, and definitely so in the context of a church.

There is little doubt that one of the key successes in the fun of starting a new ministry such as a church, is a *blessed time of prayer* that we are *forced to do*. Definitely we often feel, and rightly so, rather helpless when we are planning to start a church or ministry, and we quickly realize we are getting involved in something that is *truly beyond us*, a situation where prayer is priceless and necessary. And we see in the early first century church that is exactly what they did, in the famous "upper room," and what better source of reference about how to start a church or ministry, than the original church, 2,000 years ago! *Acts 1:14 "They all joined together constantly in prayer, along with the women and Mary the mother of Jesus, and with his brothers."*

204

17. 开展新事工的乐趣

作为建立辛城教会的长老之一，我在教会历史上曾*七次*担任代任牧师，而且每次看起来我们都好像创办了一间新教会，我可以一次又一次重温那种兴奋和乐趣。我说有趣，是因为它确实*很有趣*。这七次中的第一次发生在 50 年前的 1970 年，那时我们开始建教会；后来一次在创办青年事工时，一次在开始英文崇拜聚会时；还有另外几次当传道同工们离开以参与其他事工时，我不得不在他们离开后顶替一年或更长时间。所以从某种意义上讲，我很荣幸有机会帮助开展许多"从零或几乎从零开始"的事工。事实上，我相信无论是什么工作，开始的时候都一定会经历兴奋和快乐的时光，教会的事工也如此。

毫无疑问，要体验开展像教会那样的一项新事工的乐趣，关键之一就是要有一段*幸福的祷告时间*，那是我们*不得不做*的一件事。当我们计画开展一间教会或事工时，我们肯定会、也理应感到无助。我们很快意识到我们正在参与一件*真正超越我们能力*的事情。在这种情况下，祷告是无价和必要的。我们在一世纪初的教会中看见，这正是他们在著名的"楼上房间"中所做的事。对于如何创建教会或事工，有什么参考依据比 2,000 年前的原始教会更好！"*这些人同着几个妇人和耶稣的母亲马利亚，并耶稣的弟兄，都同心合意地恒切祷告。*"（*使徒行传一 14*）

Raising the Next Generation
to Serve
兴起新一代服事

In fact, when we started planning for the church, all kinds of people started getting interested, for various reasons. Some people liked the concept of church because they felt that it would be a good thing for the Chinese community, and be a force to draw the Chinese community together. Others thought that we could become a good charitable organization, again for the Chinese community that we derived from. But reading systematically and weekly from the Book of Acts, which records the beginnings of the first church in great detail, we were quickly reminded that the purpose of the church is to be God's representative on earth, the *gospel is key to its purpose*, and we should not lose our bearings and be distracted by many other secondary needs and concerns. *Matthew 28:19-20: "Therefore go and make disciples of all nations, baptizing them in the name of the Father and of the Son and of the Holy Spirit, and teaching them to obey everything I have commanded you. And surely I am with you always, to the very end of the age."*

So, in a very *magical* way, as we prayed every week, those people who just liked to talk, especially about their "pet reasons" for the church to be started, became quite disinterested in praying to find God's will specifically for our church. Slowly they drifted away from the regular weekly prayer meetings, and we were left with a *core group of believers* that were very strong in their belief system, and serious about seeking God's will for the church. We realized that this was really central to forming a good church, a *core group* of faithful dedicated prayer warriors, and we had gotten them, maybe somewhat "accidentally" (or so it seemed to us) the first time!

One good thing about starting something new is people tend to be *quite enthusiastic*, especially when they are coming in truly at the *ground level*. So, I always remind people, that the natural excitement and enthusiasm should not be wasted. Indeed, we discovered with each new venture, the enthusiasm gave us often that extra "oomph" to hang in there, even at times that were a bit difficult. Sometimes I would hear a bit of grumbling, that we are really working too hard, but to me that was refreshing, and even more encouragement that we were on the right track. Being tired when doing the

事实上，当我们开始计画建立教会时，由于种种原因，各种各样的人都开始对此感兴趣。有些人喜欢教会的概念，因为他们认为这对华人社区是一件好事，会成为凝聚华人社区的力量。其他人认为我们可以成为一个好的慈善组织——同样是为了华人社区着想，我们都是源自那个社区。但是，有系统地每周阅读使徒行传中有关第一间教会成立的详尽记载后，我们很快就想起，教会的目的是成为上帝在地上的代表，*福音才是教会成立的关键*，我们不应该失去方向，被许多其他次要的需求和关注分散了注意力。*"所以，你们要去，使万民作我的门徒，奉父、子、圣灵的名给他们施洗。凡我所吩咐你们的，都教训他们遵守，我就常与你们同在，直到世界的末了。"（马太福音二十八 19-20）*

就是这样，十分*奇妙*地，当我们每周祷告，那些只是喜欢谈论、特别是对于建立教会有他们"钟爱的理由"的人，对于通过祈祷来寻求上帝给予我们教会的旨意就变得不感兴趣，渐渐地不再参加每周的定期祷告会。结果留下了*一群核心信徒*，他们的信仰体系非常坚固，并且认真地寻求上帝对教会的旨意。我们意识到要建立一间好教会，由忠心委身的祈祷战士所组成的*核心小组*真的很重要。我们第一次得到他们的时候可以说是有点"偶然"（或者给我们的感觉是这样）！

教会初创时规模总是很小，然后逐渐成长。那就像一个神奇的配方，事实也的确是这样。参与其中并看着它成长。早期的儿童和青少年事工，就是好例子。
The church always begins small and grows. It is like a magic formula, which it is. Jump in and see it grow. Like the early children and youth program.

right thing should be a joy, and later on, when we look back at the battles fought, we can relish the experience even more. *Galatians 6:9: "Let us not become weary in doing good, for at the proper time we will reap a harvest if we do not give up."*

Having some good books of reference about how to start a church, and not repeat the usual mistakes, is helpful. But I always remind people that we already have *the greatest Book* available, and it has *clear instructions*, guidelines and even the history of the early church to illustrate actually what happens. It's difficult to beat that! Theory and practice are there for our edification. It's good to read the Book regularly together as a team, and discuss how it could apply to our setting, and we are always amazed how wonderfully appropriate it is, even after 2,000 years. Every time we read the exciting events of the first century initial church, especially in the Book of Acts and the Epistles of Paul, we are just impressed to see how *history repeats* itself again and again, all over the world. And it gives us a truly correct perspective to put our own church in the setting of the greater kingdom of God, so that we do not go too far astray. Other books could be useful *technically* as a guide, but I've never found them to be as foundationally solid as the original; of course. *Acts 2:42: "They devoted themselves to the apostles' teaching and to fellowship, to the breaking of bread and to prayer."*

With the *core team prayer meeting regularly every week*, we found the rhythm, speed and momentum were just right. We had the week to think through some issues, and we could come back the following week to see our fellow believers and coworkers, solidly in a team praying, thinking, planning, deciding. You could really say that it was quite a *heady time* and, if we were not careful, it could indeed all go to our head, because of the excitement. In order to reduce our running on head drive, we needed to be truly *humble* before God, by making sure that the core meeting was actually focused really on prayer. If I were to "do it again," I would like to "enhance" the process: in more recent years, during prayers for major matters, I have been encouraged by the use of intermittent prayers during the prayer meeting, pausing to pray

开始新事物的好处是人们往往*非常热情*，特别是当他们真正从*入门水准*加入的时候。因此我总是提醒他们，不应该浪费由衷的兴奋和热情。事实上，我们发现对于每一项新的事工，即使遇到一点困难的时候，热情往往给我们带来额外的活力，让我们坚持下去。有时我会听到一点抱怨：我们真的工作得太用功了，但对我来说这是令人耳目一新的，甚至更加鼓励我们走在正确的轨道上。在做正确的事情时感到疲倦应该是一种快乐，之后再回顾打过的仗时，我们可以更加津津乐道。*"我们行善，不可丧志；若不灰心，到了时候就要收成。"（加拉太书六 9）*

有一些关于如何建立教会、不去重复常犯的错误的好书作为参考，是有帮助的。但我总是提醒人们，我们已经有了那本*最好的书*，它有*明确的指示*和准则，甚至有早期教会的历史来阐明实际的情况。其他的书很难胜过它！当中有理论和实践启迪我们。整个团队定期一起阅读这本书，并讨论它如何可以套用在我们的处境中，是很好的。我们总是感到惊讶，即使是在 2,000 年之后，它还是那么切合我们的处境。特别是在使徒行传和保罗的书信中，记载了第一世纪初期教会那些激动人心的事件，每次我们阅读这些事件时，我们都会看到*历史*如何在世界各地一次又一次地*重演*。它为我们提供了一个真正正确的观点，把我们自己的教会置于上帝更大的国度中来看，这样我们就不会步入迷途。其他书籍可能在*技术上*是有用的指南，但我从未发现它们能像这本原始书籍一样有坚固的根基。*"〔门徒〕都恒心遵守使徒的教训，彼此交接，擘饼，祈祷。"（使徒行传二 42）*

每周定期召开核心团队的祷告会，让我们发现节奏、速度和动力都恰到好处。我们有一周的时间来思考一些问题，可以在接下来

for each important item on the agenda, as the issue comes up: thus, prayer can truly penetrate and permeate the meeting, and isn't an "ceremonial" afterthought. *Matthew 6:33: "But seek first his kingdom and his righteousness, and all these things will be given to you as well."*

Jesus had 12 apostles, and he led and taught them, and I could say drove them in the right direction, to ultimately set up the church, and to change the world. It was a *very small team*, not an army. It was a fragile team, who scattered in fear when Jesus was crucified. It wasn't a team of high powered executives, just "ordinary" country folk. But they were faithful and obeyed his Great Commission, to reach to the ends of the world, knowing full well that Christ had promised that He would be with them, even to the ends of the world. And to top it all off, He precipitated the church, strategically, by *leaving them*! "All they had to do," He said, was to remember what He had taught them, and to listen to the Spirit of God, which sounds simple enough. You might now agree in hindsight, it has been a wonderful prescription. Word and Spirit, you really can't beat that! And one third of the world proves it! *John 14:16: "And I will ask the Father, and he will give you another advocate to help you and be with you forever--*

But wait, you say, people do *come and go*; what happens when one of the key leaders decides to leave? Well, this really happened to us several times, and it was tough I must say, at least initially. We had 3 elders initially for our fledgling church, with 2 of the elders entrusted with the actual organization of the church. Our first shock was that the senior elder-leader of the church, was called to go to a small town in Florida by his company, and suddenly I was left holding the organization bag alone, or so I felt. Then, later when this same elder returned, we were greatly encouraged that he decided, after a few years, to take early retirement and assume full-time elder responsibilities, as de facto minister. At this point, I thought that this would really stabilize the church.

But, after only a couple of years, to my shock again, he got up at a prayer meeting and declared that he had received the calling from God, to

的一周见到我们的信徒和同工，整个团队一起祈祷、思考、计画和做决定。真的可以说这是一个非常*令人兴奋的时刻*，如果我们不小心，兴奋的感觉确实可以冲昏我们的头脑。为了减低我们靠自己的头脑运转的机会，我们需要在上帝面前做到实实在在地*谦卑*，确保核心团队的会议真正专注于祷告。如果我可以"重来一次"，我想"强化"这个过程：近年来在为重大事情祷告时，令我感到鼓舞的是，我们会在祷告会期间使用间歇性祷告，即是当问题出现时就停下来，为议程中的每个重要项目祷告。因此，祷告可以真正地渗透到会议中，而不是事后的"仪式"。*"你们要先求他的国和他的义，这些东西都要加给你们了。"*（马太福音六 33）

耶稣有 12 个使徒，祂带领并教导他们朝着正确的方向拓展，最终建立教会、改变世界。这是一支*非常小型的团队*，不是一支军队。这是一支脆弱的团队，当耶稣被钉在十字架上时，他们因恐惧而四散。它不是一个由高级管理人员组成的团队，他们只是"普通"的*乡下人*。但是他们忠心并服从祂的大使命，走到地极，因为他们清楚地知道基督已经应许他们，即使到了世界的尽头，也与他们同在。最重要的是，祂通过*离开他们*而战略性地促成了教会！祂说，他们必须做的，只是要记住祂教给他们的东西，并听从圣灵，这听起来很简单。你现在可能会事后同意，这是一个很棒的处方。上帝的话和圣灵，你真的无法击败！世界三分之一的人证明了这一点！*"我要求父，父就另外赐给你们一位保惠师，叫他永远与你们同在。"*（约翰福音十四 16）

但是等一等，你说人们*来来去去*，当其中一位关键领导人决定离开时会发生什么事？好吧，这真的发生在我们身上好几次了，而且我必须说，至少在最初的阶段是很棘手的。最初我们的新兴教会

proceed to ministry on the West Coast. The transition happened within only a few months, and suddenly I was left holding the bag again, at that time, as the only remaining elder, since the third elder had retired. On both these occasions, during a time when the church was still kind of wobbly, it seemed to me like we were practically starting a church all over again. But actually, what happened was quite amazing. The brothers and sisters all *suddenly woke up*, and realized that the church was really all of us, and so if the leading elder left, that meant that many of the brothers and sisters had to now wake up, and help out. Which was what happened, and I thought it became a great way to *mobilize the entire church*! So after about 6 to 12 months, praise the Lord, it seemed like everything was back in shape again. Such are the amazing ways of God. *1 Peter 2:5: "You also, as living stones, are being built up a spiritual house, a holy priesthood, to offer up spiritual sacrifices acceptable to God through Jesus Christ."*

Each time, when starting all over again, it is likely good that each congregation seeks what *special vision and goal* that God might have for us. God put us on this earth for a good reason, and each one of us is here for a special reason. So it stands to reason that each congregation might have a *special role to play*. We have to *start somewhere*, and *focusing* helps us to do something well, rather than trying to do too many things that we cannot handle. Even Jesus had only 12 disciples that he trained in Galilee and Judea, and He personally did not travel beyond these regions except for the adjacent Samaria. And His focus was initially among the Jews, so we can assume that trying to focus on our strengths, gifts and opportunities is a very sensible first approach. *Acts 1:8: "But you will receive power when the Holy Spirit comes on you; and you will be my witnesses in Jerusalem, and in all Judea and Samaria, and to the ends of the earth."*

And of course what better reassurance can we have, when we know that, as the early church, we have *the Lord with us*, as He promised He would be with us *to the ends of the earth*. He will be with us as we start the church, He will be with us when we grow the church, and He will be with us as we send

有三位长老，其中两位长老被委任为传道领导。我们的第一个打击是，教会的资深长老兼领导，被他的公司派了去佛罗里达州的一个小镇，突然间我感觉孤立无援。然后，这位长老回来了，几年后他决定提前退休并承担全职的长老职责，相等于我们的牧师，给我们极大的鼓舞。当时，我认为教会真的能够稳定下来了。

但是仅仅几年之后，我再次感到震惊：在一个祷告会上全职的长老站起来宣告，他接受了上帝的呼召，继续前往西海岸开展事工。过渡期只有短短的几个月，我突然要再次单独接手，因为第三位长老退休了，我是当时剩下的唯一一名长老。这两个情形都是在教会仍然摇摆不定的时候出现，在我看来我们几乎是重新开始建立一间教会。但实际上所发生的事情真是太神奇了。弟兄姐妹们*突然觉悟*，意识到教会其实是我们所有人的，如果带领的长老离开了，就意味着许多弟兄姐妹现在必须觉醒，帮忙解决问题。事情就是这样发生了，我也认为这是*动员整个教会*的好方法！所以大约 6 到 12 个月后，赞美主，似乎一切都恢复到良好的状态。这就是上帝惊人的行事方式。*"你们来到主面前，也就像活石，被建造成为灵宫，作圣洁的祭司，借着耶稣基督奉献上帝所悦纳的灵祭。"*（*彼得前书二 5*）

每一次重新开始时，每个会友都去寻求上帝可能给我们的*特殊愿景和目标*，这是件好事。上帝把我们放在地球上是有祂的理由的，我们每个人都有特殊的理由来到这里。因此，说每个会友都可以*发挥特殊的作用*，是合理的。我们必须从*某处开始*，*专注*有助我们做好一些事情，而不是试图做太多我们无法处理的事情。即使是耶稣也只有 12 个门徒，祂在加利利和犹太地区训练他们，自己也没有走出过这些区域，只有相邻的撒马利亚例外。祂最初只是聚焦于犹

our young and old all over the world for Him! What better incentive is there in any work, when we know that God's love and joy are with us, every step of the way? I really cannot think of *any other* venture in this world that can give us as much excitement and joy. And this can apply for any new venture we have in the church, such as starting a new youth group, new college group, new English congregation, new branch church, new church in Thailand, new church in China, etc. etc. Every time we begin a new venture, we begin this process again, with joy and adventure! *Matthew 28:20b: "And surely I am with you always, to the very end of the age."*

在辛辛那提事奉主 47 年，现在到了开始新旅程的时间了。
After 47 years in Cincinnati, serving the Lord, it is finally time to move on.

太人身上，所以我们可以假设，专注于我们的优势、才能和机遇，是非常明智的第一步。"*但圣灵降临在你们身上，你们就必得着能力，并要在耶路撒冷、犹太全地，和撒马利亚，直到地极，作我的见证。*"（*使徒行传一 8*）

像早期教会一样，我们知道有*主与我们同在*，祂应许与我们同在，*直至地极*——还有比这个更好的确据吗？我们开始创办教会时，祂将与我们同在；我们的教会成长时，祂将与我们同在；我们为祂将年轻和年长的信徒差派到世界各地时，祂将与我们同在！我们知道无论要做的是什么工作，每一步都有上帝的爱和欢乐与我们同在——还有比这个更好的推动力吗？我真的想不出这个世界上会有*任何其他*事业，可以给我们带来那么多的兴奋和喜悦。这可以套用在我们教会中任何新的事工上，例如开办新的青年团体、大学团体、英语崇拜、分堂、在泰国和中国的新教会等等。每次我们开始新的事工，都带着喜乐和冒险精神展开这个过程！"*我就常与你们同在，直到世界的末了。*"（*马太福音二十八 20 下*）

翻译：Hongyan

18. Critical Mass

The English-speaking College Group at our ethnic church had been dwindling steadily from 5 or 6 to zero, and everyone was getting discouraged. It looked rather hopeless, especially as we knew that any college group was often one of the more difficult ones to maintain unless it was located close to a college campus. And, the college-age group in ethnic churches usually presented additional challenges.

Older members of the ethnic church preferred services in their own ethnic language, which naturally "limited their church options". College-age adults were usually predominantly or even only English-speaking, with many alternative options. They were "no longer kids", and often felt they had now "outgrown" the mother church of their childhood and youth, and even possibly their particular ethnicity. They had gotten used to multi-ethnic Christian fellowships and services in college, a relatively new experience and atmosphere for most of them, and they had probably grown to like it. Now having independence and mobility, they no longer necessarily felt any "allegiance" to their mother ethnic church. Most were certainly more American than Asian, and thus "Asian" church life was at some point even counter-cultural to them.

With all this in mind, knowing the challenges, I prayed about it, and asked the elder-ministers' group for permission to help restart the "college/ young adult" program. Partly because I loved to work with young people, and partly because I had previously helped out with this group. Further, I had always been keenly aware of *"critical mass"* in each ministry, and sensed that there was some ... way to help revive the group if we bore that concept firmly

18. 临界数量和群聚效应

我们中文教会里的英文大学生小组从五到六个人慢慢地减少到一个都不剩，我们对此都感到沮丧。我们觉得这项事工可能是没有希望了，因为我们知道除非我们的教会离大学很近，否则大学生小组是特别难以维持的。而在族群教会里维持一个大学生小组更是难上加难。

族群教会里年长的会友希望用他们的母语崇拜，这很自然对"教会的选项设了限"。读大学的年轻人们绝大部分是说英语的，其中又有很多是只说英语的。他们有很多讲英文的教会可以选择。他们"不再是孩子"。他们通常觉得自己已经长大，小时候的母会，甚至他们的原生族裔，已不再适合他们。他们已习惯在大学里参与多族裔的基督教团契和崇拜。这种经验和气氛对他们大部分人都比较新，而他们也入境随俗地开始喜欢上了。在得到独立与行动自由后，他们不再觉得有"义务"留在少数族裔的母会里。他们绝大部分像美国人多过像亚洲人，因此，"亚洲人"教会里的生活在某种程度上跟他们是格格不入的。

了解到这一切，亦知道有什么困难和挑战，我向上帝祷告，请求长老及传道人们给我一个机会重启"大学生/年轻成人"的项目。原因之一是我热爱与年轻人一起事奉，也因为我曾经在这个小组中帮过忙。再者，我向来清楚知道*群聚效应*对各项服事的重要性，

in mind. The logic was that each ministry needed a certain essential "critical" number of participants, and anything less than that was usually liable to fail. In analyzing the college group problem, I felt this could be one major reason for its demise.

And, with my highly academic research background, I also sort of wanted to "test this hypothesis". I began to think of a list of 7 or so people that I could invite for this "research study". I prayed for each one of the 7, approached each one, usually over coffee or lunch, and gave them a simple proposal. I explained the plan that I would personally commit to recruit a minimum of 7 people, a biblical number anyway. But the key condition was that each person recruited, including me, had to make a solid commitment *not to leave* the group for at least one year. *Critical* also meant each one was critical! Rain or shine, they had to commit to come every week, unless they were out of town. I excluded people who often traveled out of town from this "core group", since their attendance would be inconsistent.

I was pleasantly surprised when, within a month, I got firm commitments from 7 college folk, and off we went! Having 7 meant that even if one person was sick or had to travel, we still had at least 6 people, and 6 people "looked like" a real group. When people visited, "looks" were the first *critical* impression, and quite *critical* to their decision to return or not. Frankly, 3 or 4 people really did *not* look like a group at all. And if I were in a visitor's shoes, I might not return either!

But 6 or 7 indeed *seemed* like a real group! And so, newcomers began to return, and actually stayed, which presto, meant our mass actually began to *increase*. Soon, we were 10 people, even 15 people normally, and 20 people during the summer season, when college kids came back to town.

There was now a "virtuous cycle" of increased numbers promoting *more* people, rather than a "vicious cycle" of fewer people creating even fewer. The moral of the story is there is often some kind of a "magical" critical mass number, so that anything less, unfortunately, usually means the ultimate disintegration of the group! Of course, we are assuming the teaching part of

18. 临界数量和群聚效应
18. Critical Mass

觉得我们若能把这个概念发挥就还是有希望的。这个概念是说每一种事工都必须有某个"临界数量"的参与者。若不能达到那个数量，这项事工多数会以失败告终。我分析了我们大学小组的问题，觉得临界数量应该是它失败的一个主要原因。

因为我是从事学术研究的，我就想"测试我的假设"。我开始思考我可以邀请哪些人来参与这个"研究"，并列出了7个人。我为这7个人祷告，亲自和每一个人喝咖啡或吃午饭，并给他们各人一个简明的提案。我向他们说明我要招募至少7个人，7刚好是圣经里常见的数字。但主要条件是连我在内的每一个人，都必须承诺在一年内*不离开*这个小组。在群聚效应的概念中，每个人都*至关重要*！除非是有事出城，每个人都必须承诺每周都要见面，风雨无阻。我没有把常常出城的人加进这个"核心小组"内，因为他们不能稳定地每周出席。

令我惊喜的是，我在一个月内得到7个大学生的承诺，我们就这样开始了！小组有7个人，代表就算我们中间有一个人因为生病或者出城而不能来，我们仍有6个人出席。6个人聚在一起"看起来"也像是一个真正的小组。当有新人来参加聚会时，我们"看起来"如何对他们是一个*至关重要的*印象，是他们决定是否再回来参加我们的聚会的*关键*因素。老实说，3或4个人聚在一起看起来真的不像一个小组。我若是一个新人，我也大概不会想再来！

但是6或7个人*看来*就像是一个真正的小组！因此，新人开始再来并留下，转眼间我们的人数开始*增长*了。不多久我们就达到10个人，甚至15个人。而在暑假大学生回家的时期，我们小组有20个人。

我们达到了"良性循环"——增长的人数带动*更多*的人来参

219

the group is solid, without which, all bets are off (if we are allowed to bet).

Actually, I had really learned this lesson well while helping with the youth group. If there were not around 7-10 people in *each grade*, I felt the system seemed to start falling apart. Something less, say, 6 people in a grade meant, say, 3 girls and 3 boys. Which meant that if one boy was missing, there were only 2 boys left when any newcomer visited the youth group. If one of the remaining boys was "not likable", or even "offensive", there was a brewing disaster. On the first or second visit, a boy might decide quickly on arrival that he had "no friends", or might even express the teen sentiment, "there's *no one* here", and drop out just like that. Teens are very sensitive, and even though there might be lots of other kids, he's only *counting* his immediate same-age, same-sex friends as "real" kids.

Adults can barely understand this, because they seem to see "lots of kids" in the youth group, and wonder why kids think that there are not enough! If we can maintain 7-10 youth per grade, we are usually much safer and, more importantly, the youth feel much safer. I have always felt we should strive hard for this *critical mass* to be reached so that we could have a workable, healthy youth group. So, one of the goals in the group could actually be to intentionally *recruit* to reach a better number. Or look into merging with another church to achieve critical mass.

Of course, smaller numbers could still work if we simply forced all the youth into one big group, to learn to consider everyone as a friend, so there are options. But then we truly have to work extra hard to make the kids realize that. A strong youth director or minister who teaches very well and who is able to keep their focused attention can go a long way to overcome that. But it would be exhausting, and it might contribute to burn-out for him or her.

There is little question that Vacation Bible School, VBS, is one of the liveliest times of the year, but it's lively only when there is a *critical mass* of workers. If there are 50 kids, we really need 50 helpers or even 100, it is that important! There are just so many, many, jobs that are needed, going all the way from drivers, craftspeople, food people, teachers, games people,

18. 临界数量和群聚效应
18. Critical Mass

与。我们打破了因为人数不足造成成员流失的"恶性循环"。这个故事告诉我们，小组通常需要一个"神奇的"临界数量，若是不能达到那个数量，小组通常会瓦解消失！当然，我们是以小组有充实的教导内容为前提，若是没有，这一切都是没有用的。

棘手的大学生／青年小组——我们坚持达到 7 个人的*临界人数*，造成了人数增长而不是减少的*良性*循环。

The challenging college/young adult group, where *insisting* on a target *critical mass* of 7 triggered a *virtuous* cycle of increasing, as contrasted to decreasing, numbers.

事实上，我是在帮助青年小组时实实在在地学到了这个功课。如果*每一个年龄组*没有 7 至 10 个人，我觉得系统就会开始瓦解。就拿 3 个女孩和 3 个男孩的 6 人小组来说，如果其中一个男孩不能来，当新人来时我们就只剩下 2 个男孩。如果剩下的其中一个男孩"不好相处"或者是"有敌意"，就会酝酿出麻烦。来过一两次的新男孩很快就认定他在小组里"没有朋友"，甚或感觉"那里*什么人都没有*"，于是就这样离开，不再回来。青少年感觉灵敏，虽然那里可能还有许多孩子，但他只会把和他年龄相当的同性朋友*算作*"真正的"孩子。

成年人对此感到困惑，他们觉得青少年组有"很多孩子"，不

storytellers, to timekeepers and traffic people.

Without all these people, VBS doesn't run well at all, and it becomes pretty chaotic. But with all these people, with adequate critical mass, suddenly we have a remarkably harmonious, lively and inspirational VBS. So, a key part of the equation is for the coordinator to mobilize, mobilize, cajole, cajole, to find and organize everyone together, for a wonderful time!

大型的青少年小组让*每一个年龄组*都能超过临界人数。
青少年不用担心"我的小组里一个人也没有"。
A big youth group allows *each grade* to exceed critical mass levels, reducing youth anxieties of "there's no one in my youth group".

Similarly, small churches have great problems when the critical mass of a congregation of about 100 is not reached. When we think about the complexity of a church, there are so many functions that need to be handled -- ushers, musicians, chairpersons, Sunday School teachers, childcare givers, preachers, maintenance, outreach, etc. And if there are not enough people, each person holds 3 responsibilities and can easily feel overwhelmed. Beginning a church, with its smaller numbers, is definitely not easy, but the hope that keeps the congregation going is that within a finite time, numbers might reach about 100.

We experienced this critical mass problem often in our Chinese church, likely mostly because of our Midwestern location. Even when the church had grown to 300 to 500 people, the sub-population that preferentially spoke *English* was actually quite small. So, throughout the 25 years or so of its life, as we tried hard to build up an English-speaking congregation, which we named, aspirationally, the "All Nations Congregation", it was a constant uphill battle. In spite of the fact that we had solid biblically-minded ministers in

明白为什么孩子们总是觉得人数不够！我们若能维持每个年龄组有7至10个孩子，那些小组通常就比较安全，而且更重要的是孩子们也觉得安全。我向来觉得我们应该致力达到这个*临界数量*，这样就可以有一个健康、能够在当中工作的青少年小组。因此，小组的目标之一应该是*招募*组员以达到数量，或者尝试和其他教会的小组一起聚会来达到临界数量。

当然，若人数较少，我们也可以把所有青少年聚集起来作为一个组，让他们学习与每个人做朋友。这是一个选项，不过我们得特别努力让所有孩子都明白这一点。虽然一个有能力、很会教导、能令孩子专注的青少年小组主任或者传道人能有力地克服这个难题，但却需要花一段长时间，很容易令小组主任或传道人的精力透支。

假期圣经班毫无疑问是一年里其中一段最有活力的时间，前提是我们有*临界数量*的同工支持。我们若有50个孩子，就需要50个甚至100个同工。这是十分重要的！我们有太多太多的工作需要人手，如司机、手工艺老师、管食物的人、老师、游戏同工、讲故事的人、计时员，和交通管理人。

如果人手不够，假期圣经班就不能有效地进行，更可能变成一团糟。反之，如果有足够人手，达到临界数量，我们就能有一个顺利、有活力、启发人心的假期圣经课程。因此，成功的诀窍在于协调者要动员再动员，哄骗再哄骗，物色对象并把所有人组织在一起，造就一段美好的时光！

同样地，小教会的会众人数若达不到100人的临界数量，就会出现大问题。教会里有许多复杂的行政工作，如招待、诗班、主日学教师、孩童照顾者、组长、传道人、维修人员、外展人员等。如果人数不够，我们可能要一人兼三职，容易让人感到不胜负荷。要

sequence, who valiantly tried to sustain and strengthen the congregation, and many volunteer leaders and helpers, it was only barely possible to get the numbers up to the 100 mark.

So, as the numbers dropped below that in the more recent last few years, it seemed that a vicious cycle did indeed happen, and with spinning down numbers, the English-speaking congregation, as I understand it, reverted to an English-speaking fellowship. There are times and seasons for everything, and maybe this noble experiment in the Midwest was destined to be a 25-year phenomenon. From informal feedback, encouragingly, those who "graduated" from this experimental phase remain serving in other, usually "white," churches, as very small Asian minorities within the All Nations Great Commission mandate.

Much larger English-speaking Asian/Chinese populations on the West or East Coast or in major metropolitan areas provide a much greater potential, I'm sure, for English-speaking congregations in Chinese churches to achieve critical mass. An alternative All Nations approach might be to flip the script. A model that I have recently been involved in, during these last few years in Seattle, is a huge 4,000-member so-called "white church," which recently has included an autonomous small new 60-member Chinese congregation within its physical confines. Plus autonomous Hispanic, African, and Asian Indian congregations. I think this approach could be a much more viable multi-ethnic model. Newer immigrants who are comfortable speaking and listening to Chinese can attend the Chinese church. At the same time, the English-speaking younger ethnic Chinese adults (and youth and children) could, in theory, merge well with other English-speaking young Asians as well as non-Asians, as part of the larger multi-ethnic English-speaking church, as a not-so-minor minority.

100 seems to be a good biblical number. Remember Jesus told the famous story of the good shepherd with 100 sheep. The shepherd was able to recognize that he had lost one sheep at the end of the day, and quickly went out to find it. I can imagine if the flock were a lot larger, his job of keeping

18. 临界数量和群聚效应
18. Critical Mass

从极少数人开始建立一个教会，是很不容易的。但是若希望教会持续下去，就要在限定的时间内增长到 100 人。

我们的华人教会就经常经历到这个临界人数的问题，这很可能是因为我们位于美国的中西部。即使在 300 到 500 人的教会里，偏向讲*英语*的人数实际上很少。因此在我们教会大约 25 年的时间里，即使我们努力要建立一群英语会众，并且满怀热心地给它起名为"万国会众"，但我们仍然一直如逆水行舟一般。即使我们不断有着坚实、以圣经为中心的传道人英勇地试着维持并强化这个会众，加上许多志愿领袖和帮手的努力，我们也只是勉强达到了 100 人这个指标。

近年这个人数降到 100 人以下之后，人数下降的恶性循环好像开始了。按照我的理解，人数下降的英语会众缩减成了英语团契。万物都有定时，也许这个在中西部进行的理想实验注定是一个维持 25 年的现象。让我感到鼓舞的是，我私下听到消息，那些从这个实验中结业的人，仍然在其他多数是"白人"的教会里服事，以非常少数的亚裔身份，实践向万国传福音的大使命。

如何达到临界人数是我们的一个挑战：中西部一个典型的族群教会试着达到临界人数，以建立一个青少年和英语会众。建立新教会的好处是，每个人都知道必须亲力亲为。当每个人的工作都是必要的时候，任何一个人都很难偷懒。就这样，教会里的每一个人都倍受激励。

It is always a challenge to achieve critical mass levels: a typical Midwestern ethnic church, trying to achieve crucial numbers for the budding youth and English-speaking congregation. The good thing in developing a new church is that everyone realizes they are clearly in an "all hands on deck" mode for ministry. It is difficult to slack off when everyone is clearly needed, and it energizes the whole church.

track of his sheep would be a lot more difficult (unless the Shepherd was actually Jesus!). Even Moses' father-in-law, Jethro, suggested dividing the people of Israel into groups of 100, for Moses' sanity and for better time management. And we all know of the hyper-efficient Romans, from the Roman *centurion* stories in the bible. 100 as an organizational critical number.

Before that number is reached, creative opportunities are available to achieve critical numbers. For example, by working with another small church congregation to share functions, facilities or workers in order to achieve critical numbers. Clearly, together there is strength. In the beginning of our church, we met in an "American" church, the Northern Hills Bible Chapel, for 14 years. The church was most generous in providing the space for us without charge; of course, we made contributions in appreciation. This arrangement also allowed us to join their children's program, especially their Vacation Bible School. We used their facilities extensively, while adjusting our meeting times to fit theirs. It wasn't ideal, but it did allow us to survive well for the first difficult 14 years. We treasured this wonderful opportunity to work with others from a very different background, and definitely we learned a lot. And, even though we did not conceptualize it that way, we were likely already experimenting with some kind of All Nations approach.

I think a key lesson is that it's really important to be humble, and to

我们的医疗事工在工作开始的时候赠送了 100 只羊给山里的乡民。这提醒了我们牧人寻羊的比喻——有 100 只羊的牧人关心那只遗失的羊。100 也是教会（羊群）人数的一个好数字。

Giving away 100 sheep in the first days of our medical mission, MSI, to a mountain tribal group. A reminder to us of the parable of the shepherd's concern for the one lost sheep, from his flock of 100. A good number for a church (sheep) congregation also.

18. 临界数量和群聚效应
18. Critical Mass

在美国西岸或东岸或大都市有着更多讲英语的亚洲或华人人口。华人教会在那些地方建立英语会众,我肯定有更大机会达到临界人数。近几年来我在西雅图一所有 4,000 多人的所谓的"白人教会"参与了另一种形态的万国事工。我们近来在会堂里新开了约 60 人的华人独立的崇拜。我们另外还有拉美裔、非裔和印度裔的各自独立的崇拜。我觉得这样是比较可行的多族裔模式。讲中文的新移民可以参加中文崇拜,同时,讲英语的较年轻的华裔成人(或者是青少年或孩童)在理论上可以轻易融入其他说英语的亚裔和非亚裔族群,并成为多族裔英语大教会里为数不少的小众。

"100"好像也是一个好的圣经数字。我们记得耶稣讲过好牧人和 100 只羊这个广为人知的故事。在一天结束的时候,牧人发现他丢失了一只羊,就赶紧去寻找。可以想像如果他的羊群数量更多,他将很难追踪每一只羊。(除非这个牧人是耶稣!)就连摩西的岳父叶忒罗也建议把以色列人分成 100 人一组,让摩西更好管理。我们也从罗马人*百夫长*的圣经故事知道,超高效率的罗马人用 100 人作为组织的临界人数。

假如还未能达到这个人数,我们可以尝试一些有创意的方法,例如和其他小教会合作分担工作、场地,以及同工来达到临界人数。团结就是力量。我们教会刚开始的时候就是在一个名为北丘圣经教会的"美国人"教会里聚会了 14 年。那个教会很慷慨地免费让我们使用场地。当然,我们也因感恩而奉献。我们因此也参与了他们的孩童活动,特别是他们的假期圣经课程。我们很频繁地使用他们的场地,同时因应他们的时间表来调动我们的聚会时间。虽然这不是理想的聚会方式,但却让我们度过了那艰难的 14 年。我们珍惜这个宝贵的机会,跟其他与我们的背景截然不同的人合作,也从那

learn to borrow talents where we can. The greater Church of God has lots of talents, and when we tapped those (All Nations) talents, it benefitted the entire church. Especially for our developing youth group, it was essential to be able to recruit many non-Asian young men and women to help out as counselors, so that we could achieve critical counselor numbers.

As described in greater detail elsewhere, we made friends with several outstanding churches that had great youth programs, and "borrowed" their talent. These young people themselves were blessed by this experience (usually their first) of working in cross-cultural ministry. Thus inspired and encouraged, some even went on to the mission field. Basically, whenever we had holes in our system, we did not feel ashamed or reluctant to recruit from "other" churches to fill those holes, to reach critical mass level, definitely "critical" for the ministries, as the word implies. I suppose there is nothing really magical about actual numbers. They are just convenient guides. God can work with any number. In fact, there were only 12 apostles, who started a revolution which now numbers 2 billion people. So, Jesus felt 12 was critical for His ministry; otherwise He would have recruited more. Or, one (David) was the right number against the giant Goliath and his army. As we like to say, one plus God is huge, and *beyond* critical. Still, numbers are fun, so ponder on them a bit.

里学到很多。虽然我们没有刻意这样设想,但我们很可能已经实验了一种万国同工的方式。

我认为我们要学习的一项重要的功课是必须谦卑,学习借用我们找得到的才能和资源。上帝的大教会有众多有才干的人,当我们运用这些来自万国的才干,整个教会都能得益处。特别是当我们发展青少年小组时,我们需要招募许多非亚裔青年作为辅导员,我们在辅导员方面才能达到临界人数。

就如我在别处提过的,我们与好些有着很好的青少年事工的杰出教会成为好友,并"借助"他们的才干。这种参与跨文化事工的经验(往往也是他们的第一次体验)也令那些年轻人蒙福。他们得到激励和鼓舞,有些人甚至走进了宣道工场。当我们的系统有漏洞的时候,我们并不感到丢脸,也不会不愿意寻求"别的"教会帮助,填补那些漏洞,来达到临界人数。这一点对事工肯定是不可或缺的。我认为数目本身并没有神奇功效,它只是一个方便的指标。上帝可以使用任何数目。事实上,只有12个使徒就开展了一场革命,到现在牵涉了20亿人。所以,耶稣认为12个人是祂事工的临界人数,若非如此,祂应该会招募更多人。又例如要对抗歌利亚和他的军队,"一"(大卫)就是合适的数目。就如我们常说,一个人加上帝就是大数目,远*超过*任何一个临界点。即便如此,数字还是很有趣,值得我们思考多一点。

**翻译:Edison Lim

19. We Didn't Hire Them, So We Can't Fire Them

Many people seem to think that we could just "hire" a minister to solve the problems in our church. I hear this comment often, and I'm rather uncomfortable with the word "hire" and its implications. In our church, we have an unusual tradition, "since we don't hire ministers, we cannot fire them."

This sounds very strange at first, and you might say, "What if the minister turns out not to be a "good" one?"

Well, why didn't we have a good minister? Did we pray enough? Did we seek God's will enough? The church founders had a basic simple assumption that *God would provide* us leaders or pastors in His time. It wasn't the conventional "hire a pastor" approach. We could be on the lookout for good leaders but we trusted God would be the prime force to send us a leader. Idealistic maybe, but it lasted more or less during my decades at the church. We felt that the church should not be an employment agency for pastors, but should be more like a family. We "don't hire", nor are we supposed to "fire" our parents or our spouses.

So, a lot of times the issue in practical terms is how we go about trying to find a minister. If we try to use secular ways of evaluating the skills and competency of the minister, we may downplay the spiritual qualities, the inner strengths of the minister. But if we go about it in the same way that we are supposed to seek the will of God in finding our spouses, knowing full well that we will never divorce, then in searching for the right minister, we will

19. 没雇用，没解雇

很多人认为我们只需要"雇用"一位全职传道人就可以解决我们教会的问题。每次听到这样的提议，都会对"雇用"这个字眼和它的含意感到不自在。我们教会有个不寻常的传统："我们不雇用传道人，所以就不能解雇他们"。

乍听之下这很奇怪。也许你会问，如果后来发现传道人"不太理想"，怎么办？

我们应该自问：为什么我们没有一位好的传道人？我们有没有做足够的祷告？我们在祷告中有没有寻求上帝的旨意？教会的创立者有一个基本的信念，认为*上帝会*在合适的时间为我们*提供*领袖或牧师。而不是用社会中常见的方式去"雇用牧师"。我们可能正在寻找一位好的领袖，但我们相信上帝才是成就此事的主要力量。也许有些理想主义，但这种形式在我几十年的教会经历中，始终延续着。我们认为教会不应成为牧师的雇主，而应更像一个家庭。我们不会"雇用"也不应"解雇"我们的父母或是配偶。

牧师是宝贵的，师母是无价的。要爱和珍惜他们。
The Pastor is precious, the Pastor's Wife is invaluable. Love and cherish them.

因此，实际的问题往往是我们如何物色全职传道人。如果我们用世俗的方

be super careful to emphasize the spiritual qualities, the integrity, the long-lasting characteristics, rather than any dramatic secular "professional" skills and competencies.

In our church history, every time we looked for a minister, we took a long, long time over it, even to the point of frustration of the candidate and church members, because we understood that it was the will of God that we were seeking, and therefore we should not try to hurry the decision. We checked the background thoroughly and meticulously, and especially we valued those who have come from within our own ranks, since that we would know the person really very, very, well. All it would take is one scandal and all the good work would be destroyed.

确认上帝给我们年轻的青年组传道人的呼召——那是一个漫长的祷告过程。
Affirming God's calling for our young youth minister: it's a long, prayerful process.

But then you say that no one's perfect. So, what about the minister that really is not doing a good job? If the minister is "not doing a good job", there might be many reasons for that, including the responsibility of the congregants. It would mean that members, and especially deacons and elders should sit down together with the minister and talk it over, to figure out what the problems are. Every minister, I'm sure, wants to do his best work, and so therefore we should sit down and try to figure out how help him to do so. This is just like in a family: if any part of the family is not doing so well, we need to have a family discussion to try to fix the problem. And the problem might well be a misfit in responsibilities given to the ministers; it could be misplaced, unrealistic expectations; it could be some skill that could be enhanced. The discussion might be awkward and

法以他们的技巧和能力作为标准来甄选，就有可能忽略了属灵的品质——那是传道人内在的实力。我们选择配偶时会寻求上帝的旨意，因为清楚知道选配偶是一辈子的事，不应该离婚。如果我们以选配偶的心态来物色传道人，我们将会非常小心，特别注重属灵的品德、操守和持久的特质，而不是属世社会考虑到的"专业"技巧和能力。

在我们教会的历史中，每次物色传道人都需要很长的时间，甚至连会众和候选人都觉得无奈和沮丧。但我们都明白我们是在寻求上帝的旨意，所以不能操之过急。我们会仔细查看候选人的背景，几近到挑剔的程度。我们也特别重视在我们教会长大的候选人，因为我们会对他非常非常熟悉。将来只要有一宗丑闻，所有的努力都会功亏一篑。

你也许会说世上没有一个人是十全十美的，如果一个传道人没有好的工作表现，那又怎样？传道人"没有好的工作表现"，可能有许多原因，教会会众也可能要负上部分责任。会友、特别是执事和长老应该与传道人坐下来，找出问题的症结。我肯定任何一个传道人都希望尽力做好自己的工作。所以，我们应该一同坐下来想想有什么方法帮他。情况就像一个家庭：如果任何一位成员有问题，一家人就坐下来讨论如何解决。问题可能是我们将一些非其所长的教会事工交给了传道人；可能是一些不切实际的期望；可能是传道人可以增强一些技巧。这些讨论有时会令大家觉得尴尬或为难，但这是必经之路，也的确能产生十分理想的效果。我们以往的经验也印证了以这方法来处理会得到非常好的效果。我们的教会和传道人从来没有出现过严重的分歧，也从来没有传道人因为不愉快或愤怒而辞职。在我事奉教会 46 年来，我们也从来未"解雇"过任何一

even difficult, but addressing the problem is necessary, and it does produce some very good results. We have used this approach for many years and it has worked extremely well, so we have had no major rifts; definitely no ministers that have resigned in disgust or anger, nor have we ever "fired" any minister in all these years in all my 46 years serving the church.

Another way we try to encourage the ministers is to have regular "accountability sessions" among all the ministers and elders, since we consider elders and ministers as having similar responsibilities, except that elders usually have a "secular" job in addition to their church responsibilities. Therefore, elders and ministers can sit down together frequently to work on matters of church and personal accountability. No one is perfect, and if we come together in this way, we reinforce each other and encourage each other, in a responsible and loving manner, in the true spirit of mutual accountability.

The concept we like is that "God hires the minister", since every true minister should only come in answer to God's call. So it's "God's call", not "ours". He is the employer, not us. And so the key is to carefully seek God's will and to discern if He has truly called the minister. If the minister is employed by God, then we are simply the venue and support system. If he is employed by God and not us, we have no "power" to "fire him".

建堂 40 周年，年轻的、年长的，远近都来欢庆。

Happy 40th Anniversary of our church, young and old, from far and near.

With this "no hire, no fire" tradition, we have been able to manage a church that has grown to more than 500 people, including 100 youth, which gives us a strong foundation for the future. We truly do not have any history of major breakups and high tensions that seem to plague many (including Asian) churches. Maybe you could try this approach! Don't hire your ministers!

位传道人。

我们用来鼓励传道人的另一种方法，是所有长老和传道人定期坐下来检讨并交换意见。我们教会认为长老和传道人在牧养弟兄姐妹上的职责很相近，只是长老通常在教会外另有支薪的工作。所以，长老和传道人可以经常坐下来讨论有关教会的一般行政以及牧养的事工。没有一个人是十全十美的，假如我们能够这样相聚，就可以互相鼓励和互相劝勉，既尽责亦彼此相爱，体现互相承担的精神。

长老与传道人定期互相交通讨论，营造出彼此鼓励的气氛。
Mutual accountability sessions among elders and ministers create an encouraging environment.

我们认为是"上帝雇用传道人"，因为每个真正的传道人都应该是为回应上帝的呼召而来。因此，那是"上帝的呼召"而不是"我们的呼召"。雇主是上帝而不是我们。所以真正的重点是寻求上帝的旨意，辨别祂有没有呼召那位传道人。如果传道人是上帝雇用的，我们就只是事奉的场所和支援系统。如果雇用传道人的是上帝而不是我们，我们就"无权"来"解雇"传道人。

以这种"没雇用，没解雇"的传统，我们教会的规模增长到超过 500 人，其中有 100 名青少年，给将来教会的成长打下了一个很好的基础。在过去几十年的历史中，令许多（包括亚裔）教会受到损害的严重分裂或纷争，真的没有在我们教会里发生。或许你也能试试这种方式！别雇用你的传道人！

翻译：Tom King、Amy Zhao

About the Author

The author Reginald Tsang, is a medical doctor who specializes in premature infant care (Neonatology). He was Director of the Division of Neonatology at the Cincinnati Children's Hospital Medical Center for 15 years. He has published more than 400 scientific articles and papers related especially to infant and perinatal calcium and nutrition research. In 1994 he took early retirement to answer the call for medical missions, co-founding the Medical Services International organization to work in rural minority areas in Southwest China. In 2004 he took his second retirement to serve his home church, the Cincinnati Chinese Church where he is founding elder, serving especially in youth ministry. Professor Tsang is affectionately called "Uncle Reggie" by 3 year old kids to 70 year old adults, since he loves to chat and tell many stories related to his many travels overseas. He has logged in 3 million miles of flight travel, taught 10,000 pupil hours of English especially to Chinese village kids, and helped bring more than 5,000 short term people units to China.

Professional recognitions include: President American College of Nutrition; President Midwest Society of Pediatrics; American Academy of Pediatrics Nutrition Award; Bristol Myers Nutrition Award; Cincinnati Children's Hospital Founding Executive Director of the Perinatal Research Institute; University of Cincinnati Medical School's highest academic award, the Drake award. In all these instances he was the first Asian or Chinese American to be so recognized.

作者简介

作者曾振锚是一位专门从事早产儿护理（新生儿科）的医生。他曾在辛辛那提儿童医院医学中心担任新生儿科主任15年。他发表了400多篇科学文章和研究论文，特别专注于婴儿及围产期钙质和营养的研究。1994年，他回应医疗服务使命的呼召，提早退休，与伙伴共同成立了国际医疗服务机构，服事中国西南地区少数民族的农村。2004年，他第二次退休，回到他的母会辛辛那提华人教会（他也是该教会的创会长老），致力参与青年事工。从3岁小孩到70岁长者都亲切地称呼曾教授为"Uncle Reggie（曾叔叔）"，因为他喜欢聊天，又会讲很多他海外旅行的故事。他的飞行里数已达300万英里，教授过10,000教学时数的英语，特别是教导中国乡村的小孩子，又有份带领5,000多人次到中国参与短期海外工作。

专业认可资历：美国营养学院院长；中西部儿科学会主席；美国儿科学会营养学奖；Bristol Myers营养学奖；辛辛那提儿童医院围产期研究所创办人及执行总监；辛辛那提大学医学院最高学术奖——德雷克奖。整体来说，他是第一位得到如此认可资历的亚裔或华裔美国人。

翻译：Eileen Mok

Raising the Next Generation to Serve
兴起新一代服事

Books published by Dr. Reginald Tsang
曾振锚医生著作

1. Coffee with Uncle Reggie 与曾叔叔闲聊 1：我们的新生儿科教授
2. Science Chat with Uncle Reggie 与曾叔叔闲聊 2：与曾叔叔聊科学
3. Starting an Academic Medical Career
4. 医学学术成功起步
5. Nutritional Needs of the Preterm Infant
6. 早产儿营养需要
7. Nutrition During Infancy: Principles and Practicc
8. 婴儿营养原理与实践
9. Calcium Nutriture in Mothers and Children
10. Nutrition and Bone Development (with JP Bonjour)
11. Nutrition During Infancy
12. Nutrition in Preterm Infants: Scientific Basis and Practical Guidelines
13. Mineral Requirements of Preterm Infants
14. Textbook of Neonatal Medicine: A Chinese Perspective (with Chief Editor Victor Yu)

The author invites you to read more Uncle Reggie stories at his bilingual website: Reggietales.org.

Publishing and printing of this book is supported by YFAN Heritage Foundation. You can support this effort through USA tax deductible donations to:
YFAN heritage foundation, c/o 1002 Eastgate Dr., Cincinnati, OH 45231
Check made out to: YFAN heritage foundation, Memo line: YFAN literature mission fund

作者诚邀你登上他的双语网站，阅读更多曾叔叔的故事：Reggietales.org。

本书的出版和印刷获得 YFAN Heritage Foundation 赞助。你可以捐款支持。捐款收据可申请减免美国税项。支票请邮寄至：
YFAN heritage foundation, c/o 1002 Eastgate Dr., Cincinnati, OH 45231, USA
支票抬头：YFAN heritage foundation；备注（如适用）：YFAN literature mission fund